ROCKS IN THE CLOUDS

High-Ground Aircraft Crashes of South Wales

Edward Doylerush

MIDLAND

An imprint of
Ian Allan Publishing

Dedication

This work is dedicated to the memory of all Royal Air Force, Commonwealth and Allied airmen, including USAAF and Air Transport Auxiliary pilots who lost their lives in South Wales. Also to those military personnel and civilians who were killed in air raids. They are not forgotten.

First published 2008

ISBN (10) 1 85780 281 0
ISBN (13) 978 1 85780 281 8

Published by Midland Publishing

an imprint of Ian Allan Publishing Ltd, Hersham, Surrey KT12 4RG

North American trade distribution:
Specialty Press Publishers & Wholesalers Inc.
39966 Grand Avenue, North Branch, MN 55056
Tel: 651 277 1400 Fax: 651 277 1203
Toll free telephone: 800 895 4585
www.specialtypress.com

Printed in England by Ian Allan Printing Ltd, Hersham, Surrey KT12 4RG

Code: 0801/B3

Visit the Ian Allan Publishing website at www.ianallanpublishing.com

CONTENTS

Foreword

by Don Charlwood AM

Twenty-three years have passed since I wrote the foreword to Edward Doylerush's first book, *No Landing Place*. Since then he has become a foremost authority on the many accidents in the mountainous terrain of Wales. His research has taken him south from his home at Rowen to Mid-Wales and now, in the volume you hold, to South Wales.

My own experience of flying over Wales, both north and south, was as an RAAF navigator of a newly formed crew in worn-out Wellington 1cs in the summer of 1942. Having survived our Bomber Command tour of operations on Lancasters, I then often returned to Wales as a navigation instructor on Wellington IIIs in the summer of '43. I never lost a healthy respect for the country's rock-loaded clouds!

My first contact with Edward Doylerush came as a result of an article I wrote for *Blackwood's Magazine* in 1965. It told of a long walk I had done to Carnedd Llewelyn from Tal-y-Cafn in the summer of 1943 and my attempt to repeat the walk in 1963. In particular I had hoped in '63 to return to a remote cottage, Rowlyn Uchaf, where I had sheltered from a storm, 20 years earlier. It happened that Eddie was handed this article eleven years after I had written it – that is in 1976. Perhaps in this foreword I can summarise the chain of events that ensued.

First, to go back to 1943, I was walking alone – and feeling much alone. A fellow Lancaster navigator, a close friend who was to have come with me, had recently been killed in the Pathfinder Force. I reached Carnedd Llewelyn and rested awhile at the summit. As I turned back I saw an immense cumulonimbus cloud moving slowly from the sea up the Conwy valley, its far-off volleys of thunder audible. As I was walking in no more than RAAF battledress, I decided to find shelter as quickly as I could. As I descended I came to twin lakes and near to one of them – the

Above: Wellington 1c at 27 OTU, Lichfield, 1942. L-R, Don Charlwood, navigator, Geoff Maddern, pilot, Ted Batten, bomb-aimer, Max Burcher, wireless operator, Arthur Brewett, rear gunner. (*Don Charlwood*)

forbidding Llyn Dulyn – lay the remains of a crashed Anson. I hesitated beside it, wondering about the fate of its crew, before continuing my descent.

After passing two abandoned, roofless cottages, I came to a much lower cottage set against a hillside, above a fast flowing stream. This, I found later, was Rowlyn Uchaf, or The Upper Whirlpool. The advancing cloud had now overtaken me. As the first rain fell, I heard people conversing in Welsh inside. I called, "May I shelter please from the storm?" A man's voice replied in English, "Come on in." I went in onto a flagstone floor below a high peaked roof on which the rain now beat heavily.

Three people were in this main room. Subsequently I was to find out from Eddie that they were a farmer, William Williams, his sister and their elderly mother. My sudden appearance led to a feeling of unease. After all, it was wartime and German airmen had been shot down or crashed in the area; also the dark blue of my uniform might well have been unfamiliar.

When I explained that I was an RAAF navigator and had been walking during my leave, the farmer seemed easier. He said then, "We had a New Zealander here also."

"Walking too?"

Left: L-R, Ron Waldron, Don Charlwood and William Williams at Rowlyn Uchaf, 1979. (*Author*)

"No, he crashed in an Anson on the mountains, near the lakes. The three men with him were badly injured. He covered them with silk from their parachutes before he looked for help." The farmer's gaze moved far away. "It took him seventeen hours to come down. His hands were all torn from feeling the way. One of his eyes lay out of its socket."

How inconsequential my own arrival suddenly seemed! I asked the fate of the other men. "One lived and two died."

"And the New Zealander?"

"He, too, survived."

As I stood there, the storm eased, and silence fell. The peace and beauty of the room were borne in on me. After the life of tension I had known in Bomber Command, and the New Zealander's story, I felt a place of refuge in a crazed world. At length I tried to convey this to them. The young woman smiled gently, but said nothing. She then set the table for the evening meal and, as they sat down, she came to me with a glass of milk. I drank it and thanked them and went on my way.

For 20 years I kept recalling the tranquillity of the cottage and had a longing to revisit it. In 1963 and '64, I was in Britain interviewing aviation-experienced men, mostly RAF aircrew, for Air Traffic Control training in Australia. On both visits I attempted to reach Rowlyn Uchaf. Having failed on both occasions, I wrote the account that was handed to Eddie eleven years later. In return he told me of his plan to write of the aircraft crashes around Snowdonia. My story led him to the remains of the Anson and subsequently to contact the New Zealand pilot, Ken Archer. He gave me Ken's address and I was able to visit him in New Zealand. His eyesight was by then completely restored.

Extraordinary though Eddie's information was, it was his offer to take me to Rowlyn Uchaf that gave me hope of returning to the place I so vividly remembered. In 1979, I was back briefly in Britain. By this time, Eddie had been to the cottage himself and was able to tell me that Mrs Williams had died. He and his brother-in-law, Ron, were able to lead me to the cottage by a route much less demanding than the one I had attempted earlier. Although there was no storm this time, we arrived drenched by driving rain.

Eddie's knock at the door brought the barking of a dog from the inside. Mr Williams came out to us, holding a Border Collie by the muzzle. Eddie introduced me to him. Alas, he had no memory of me. "Do you remember the New Zealand pilot?" I asked.

"Ah yes, I remember him well, and I heard that his sight was restored." Then he added, "It may be that my sister will remember you." We went into that peaceful, flagstone-floored room with its two grandfather clocks and its great cooking range. His sister, sitting beside the stove, looked as old now as her mother had looked before her. She stood up and smiled.

"This gentleman," said Mr Williams, "says he sheltered with us 36 years ago. Do you remember him?"

She replied, "A glass of milk."

I have Eddie Doylerush to thank for this memory and to thank, also, for his books and for his and his wife Mary's many kindnesses to me and my family since 1979. It is a pleasure indeed, at the age of 91, to write this foreword to *Rocks in the Clouds*.

Don Charlwood
Warrandyte, Victoria
January 2007

Author's note: Don Charlwood was awarded the Australia Medal (AM) in 1992 for services to Australian literature. His haunting experiences in Bomber Command were relived in *No Moon Tonight*, and *All the Green Year* is a classic read in schools, to mention but two of his works. Presumably, should he ever return to Wales, he could take his seat in the Assembly! (Assembly Members are AMs).

Preface

S ome time ago, during a conversation with a wartime Spitfire pilot, he mentioned a warning given to him by his instructor before he flew over Wales for the first time. "Remember Welsh clouds have hard centres!" I had to look no further, with a little adjustment, for a title for this volume.

While researching the mid-Wales area for *Fallen Eagles*, I looked beyond to the south and logged any relevant information that came forth. During this time I made contact with Len Roberts of Brecon, who knew the Brecon Beacons like the back of his hand. Not only that, but he had assembled an extensive list of aircraft crashes across South Wales. This was as good as a supercharger to another historian.

With the interior mountainous, the many airfields were confined to the coastal strip. Air space was thus crowded, and accidents were numerous. There were collisions and ditchings in the sea with few survivors. In one instance, Wellington HX482 of 172 Squadron, pilot P/O G.C.V. Jamieson, had flown from St Athan for air testing of the ASV radar equipment being developed there. The aircraft was shot down near Swansea by the crew of an American tanker who thought it was an enemy aircraft.

It would have taken several volumes to research and detail each crash, including the many airfield and lowland ones.

In the event I extracted just the high ground incidents and from these listed any crashes with survivors.

Then began the lengthy task of locating a few men across the globe. Some, having survived a traumatic crash on a lonely mountain top, did not survive the war. It seemed so unfair. It was as well this early work was undertaken though, for, with the passage of time, many of those stalwart aviators are no longer with us. However, their vivid accounts and photographs, in which their characters shine, are.

On the way I met Hugh Trivett, Luftwaffe historian, in 1989, when we attended the reunion of two German airmen: Lothar Horras and Kurt Schlender, survivors of a Heinkel crash on Llwydmor in Snowdonia (*No Landing Place* vols 1 & 2). He advised me that a Heinkel, brought down at Newport, was the only enemy aircraft to crash on land in South Wales. Hugh has contributed the story of this Heinkel, with a personal account from correspondence with the pilot, and including a surprising sequel.

Another contributor with both a chapter and a supply of invaluable information, especially on USAAF losses, was Steve Jones of Cwmafon, near Port Talbot. I have included the story of his discovery of parts of a German aircraft on the beach to its conclusion. It is a fascinating tale. Steve also located the crash site of a B-17 Flying Fortress, and indeed the sites of several crashes on the Preseli Hills, at a time when I had obtained the pilot's own detailed account of the last flight of *Gunga Din*.

John Evans of Pembroke Dock, a founder member of the Pembrokeshire Aviation Group, was approached for information on an RAF Liberator which had also crashed on the Preseli Hills. He unstintingly provided information and photographs. His published historical works include three volumes of *Sunderland Flying Boat Queen* and details of some of the many aircraft crashes in west Wales.

Without the active participation of all these historians, and vital information and photographs from others, my work would be either very thin or non-existent. This volume is not only about aircraft. They would not have flown an inch without their pilots and crews. These airmen, RAF, Commonwealth and Allied including USAAF, were all volunteers for flying duty. The business of becoming an airman was usually much more complex and demanding than it appeared at the recruiting office. Flying turned out to be not only for fine bright days. It required crews to be aloft in all weathers, to fly across unfamiliar terrain without making unscheduled contact, and to bring the aircraft and all its occupants safely back to base. Sometimes it did not go according to plan. Weather was the downfall of many crews in this work. Inexperience, the total blackout, and misty mountains were as much an enemy as the Luftwaffe.

The writer's only flight in South Wales was during a week's summer camp at RAF St Athan with the Air Training Corps in August 1945. I was taken up in de Havilland Dominie R5924, a sleek twin-engined biplane, to fly along a coast teeming with holidaymakers. Mountains sprouted above the horizon away in the distant north. Little did I know then of the aircraft losses on those peaks.

For the sake of continuity, Welsh place names are generally used as they appeared on maps and official documents of the time. I must apologise in advance for any inaccuracies in this work, either from incorrect sources or from my own misinterpretation.

The little-known aircraft crashes in the mountains are now part of the history of Wales. I am proud to have been able to complete their story with this volume.

Acknowledgements

My sincere thanks to Don Charlwood for his memorable foreword to start this volume off. Readers will see why I asked Don for his contribution a fourth time, probably a record. Also, to his daughter Doreen for her communication skills. To the Air Historical Branch, MoD, Malcolm Brown, Alec Campbell, the Coastguards of Conwy, the librarians of Conwy Library, Malcolm Cullen, Idris Davies, Derrie Edge, Alun Evans, Mrs Eileen Gard, Danny Hickey, Rose & Chris Hitchings, Mark Hodgkiss, Mrs Jennie Howells, Rhys Jeffreys, Elis Wyn Jenkind & John Morgan of Crynant Royal British Legion, Dr D. A. Jones, Phillip Jones, Susan and Dave Jones, Don Konley in the US for finding photographs of C-47 crash survivors, George B. Callicoatte and James Sigl, ex-F/Lt Stewart Manton, Graham McNeil, Simon Parry of Red Kite, members of the Pembrokeshire Aviation Group, RAF Personnel Management Agency, Jackie Phillips, Bryn Prosser, Conwy artist Jean Morgan Roberts for my printer, Richard Shearly, South Wales Argus, David J. Smith, Mrs Nora Thomas, Mrs Morag Williams, Mrs Penny Williams, Dr David Wood and two of my grandsons, Michael Thomas and Geoffrey Wedge for their invaluable help. And a big thank you to my wife Mary, for her patience.

Edward Doylerush
Snowdonia
2007

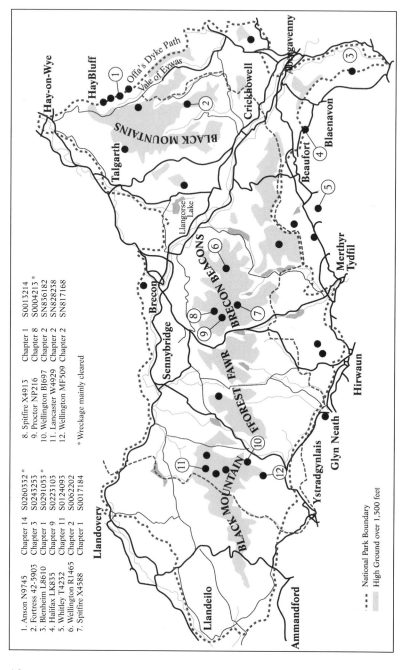

1. Anson N9745   Chapter 14   S0260332 *
2. Fortress 42-5903   Chapter 5   S0243255
3. Blenheim L8610   Chapter 1   S0291055 *
4. Halifax LK835   Chapter 9   S0223103
5. Whitley T4232   Chapter 11   S0124095
6. Wellington R1465   Chapter 2   S0062202
7. Spitfire X4588   Chapter 1   S0017184

8. Spitfire X4913   Chapter 1   S0015214
9. Proctor NP216   Chapter 8   S0004215 *
10. Wellington BJ697   Chapter 2   SN836182
11. Lancaster W4929   Chapter 2   SN828238
12. Wellington MF509   Chapter 2   SN817168

* Wreckage mainly cleared

- - - National Park Boundary

High Ground over 1,500 feet

Brecon Beacons National Park

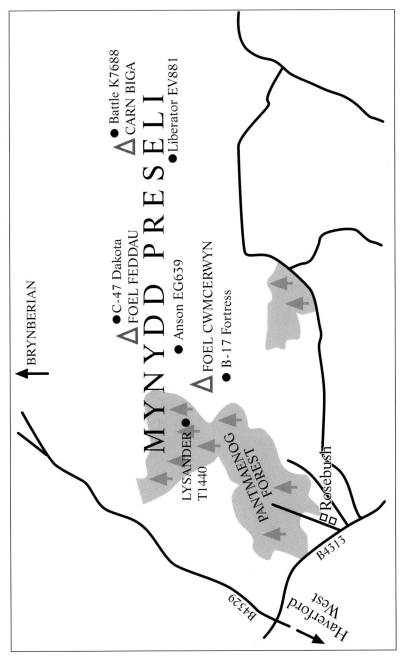

Mynydd Preseli

Part I

THE BACKGROUND

Chapter 1
The Mountains

As there is no Hadrian's, or other, wall between mid and south Wales there is some duplication of the crashes in the region and at its eastern boundary. This ensures that readers who do not have a copy of *Fallen Eagles* will not miss out. Also, some extra photographs and information have come to hand to be included.

The area of this volume follows the 'skirt' of the Old Lady of Wales as seen from space, with the mountains as the folds in the skirt. We will follow the main mountain groups from east to west, starting with the Black Mountains. These rise, with a few intervening ridges, from the plains of

Below: The Spitfire X4588 site above Gwaen Nant Ddu. (*Len Roberts*)

Left: Blenheim L8610 crashes into Garn Wen. (*Mark Hodgkiss via Danny Hickey*)

Right: The Anson L9149 site on Bannau Brycheiniog. (*Len Roberts*)

Below right: The remains of Fairey Battle K7688 on the Preseli Hills. (*Steve Jones*)

Herefordshire. Those aircrew who crashed along the first ridge were in historic country. Along the summit ridge part of a large dyke from Chepstow to Prestatyn was constructed by the order of Offa, King of Mercia, in the years AD778–796 – Offa's Dyke. The most northerly point of this ridge is 2,219 ft Hay Bluff, in shape like the prow of the *Titanic* cruising towards Hay-on-Wye.

The earliest crash in this area was an Avro Anson from No. 6 Air Observers Navigation School at Staverton, near Cheltenham. On 2 March 1940, the crew, consisting of the pilot F/Lt R. M. Nobiston and three others, Aircraftsmen W. N. Blau and J. N. Nightingale, pupil navigators, plus Mr R. M. Knight, civilian instructor, took off in Anson N9879 on a training flight. They became lost due to extensive cloud cover and deteriorating weather. The pilot was warned by radio of high ground ahead and climbed to avoid this. However, the Anson struck the mountain, just fifty feet short of the summit ridge. The pilot died from his injuries, but the rest of the crew were only slightly injured.

The range continues to the west, but is divided by the Vale of Eywas, along which flows the Afon Honddu. This larger area was the last resting place of a B-17 Flying Fortress on 16 September 1943, detailed elsewhere. The highest peak of the Black Mountains is Waunfach at 2,660 feet in the western area.

The next range, the highest in South Wales, is the Brecon Beacons, part of the Brecon Beacons National Park. The Park encompasses the first four mountain areas, including the aforementioned Black Mountains, as we move

westwards. It is a delight to those wanting a breath of fresh air and spectacular views from the former coalmining valleys to the south. The highest point, indeed, in South Wales is 2,906 feet Pen y Fan, with Waun Rhyd (2,504 feet) and the flat topped Corn Du (2,863 feet) forming a lofty triangle.

This last peak was the scene of a very early tragedy. In early August 1900, five-year-old Tommy Jones was taken by his father to see his grandparents at Cwm Llwch Farm, at the western slopes of this mountain range. Tommy managed to wander off and became lost, causing frantic searches by the family and authorities. His little body was found 29 days later on 2 September, high on Corn Du at a height of 2,250 feet. How on earth he managed to climb to this altitude will remain a mystery. A memorial stands at the spot.

This area saw few people in the war years apart from shepherds, the reason why one aircraft was missing for nearly nine months, the longest on

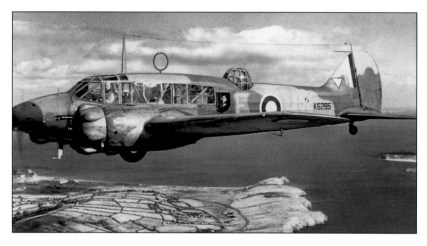

Above: Avro Anson K6285 above Pembrokeshire. (*John Evans*)

land during World War 2. On 3 November 1941, F/Sgt Gardner took off from No. 53 Operational Unit at RAF Llandow in Spitfire X4913 on an operational training exercise. He was posted as missing when he did not return. All those months later his aircraft was discovered high in a gully on the north-east face of Pen y Fan. Because of the danger of falling rocks climbers should only approach and view this site from above.

Another Spitfire, X4588 from Llandow, became detached from a formation flying exercise in bad weather on 23 May 1942. It was found around three miles south of the other Spitfire on high moorland. The pilot, Sgt D. P. Carruthers, lost his life.

There were some 63 Spitfire losses in South Wales, mostly from 53 Operational Training Unit (OTU) at RAF Llandow. Around a dozen pilots survived.

Before we move on, a mention is due of the southernmost crash in the Park, an arm of which stretches towards Pontypool. On 22 September 1940, Bristol Blenheim L8610, a twin-engined light bomber, took off from RAF Upwood in Hampshire on a cross-country training exercise. The pilot was Sgt H. Wilson, with P/O A. D. Coplestone, observer, and Sgt John November as wireless operator/air gunner.

During the flight the weather deteriorated to such an extent that the crew were forced to fly on instruments. In these conditions the aircraft

Above left: F/Sgt Ken Owens, the pilot of Anson EG639. (*Hazel Nutter*)

Above right: Sgt John Venus, the wireless operator of Anson EG639. (*Hazel Nutter*)

collided with the summit of Garn Wen with the loss of the three airmen. The pilot was the eighth and youngest child of his parents. He was the only son to survive infancy, and was greatly cherished by his parents and older sisters. His death at the age of 22 was a great shock to the family.

The next region, Fforest Fawr, takes its name from the extensive medieval hunting grounds reaching from the bare upland moorlands to the lower wooded valleys. Fan Fawr in the eastern part is the highest point at 2,409 feet, followed in the western flow of the high ridge by 2,381 feet Fan Gyhirych. A crash occurred in 1966 when bad weather, modern technology and judgement played their part. At 1326 hours on 11 February, 'V' bomber Avro Vulcan XH536, of 12 Squadron, took off from RAF Cottesmore in Rutland. After an hour's flight at 40,000 feet the aircraft descended to the Welsh stage of the UK low level route to use its TFR (Terrain Following Radar). Another Vulcan preceded them on the route. The weather forecast was a cloud base of 2,000 feet, but in actuality it was much lower than this.

The leading Vulcan reduced height to, and stayed at, 5,000 feet but XH536 continued with the low level flight pattern, and at 1510 hours it struck the summit of 1,980 feet Fan Bwlch Chwyth, spreading wreckage that was highly visible in the snow some half a mile along the ridge.

The pilot, F/Lt McDonald, and his four crewmen F/O Sutcliffe, F/Lt R. Core, F/Lt B. Waring and F/Lt E. Fuller, were killed instantly. Following a report in a local newspaper, a man on holiday in the area who had read it advised the editor that the father of one of the crew had died twenty years earlier at more or less the same spot.

The next mountain block to the west is the Black Mountain, with the highest peak being 2,630 feet Fan Brycheiniog. In the late 1930s, the RAF encouraged commercial aviation schools to train some civilians as pilots and observers, in order to reduce the time to produce aircrew should we go to war. One of these schools was situated at Hamble near Southampton. On the afternoon of 17 January 1939, Anson L9149 took off for a navigational flight to Coventry via Cardiff. The pilot was F/O E. R. N. Coombes with Aircraftsman M. Mabbott and two civilians, John MacDonald of Glasgow and L. A. Prescott of Wyken, Coventry, on board. On reaching Wales the weather deteriorated as they headed for the mountains to the north. Because of cloud and heavy rain, the pilot was flying on instruments; the aircraft was also slowly losing height.

Without warning the Anson struck high ground, the summit of 2,600 feet Bannau Brycheiniog. The aircraft was a wreck with the pilot and Aircraftsman Mabbott badly injured and trapped inside. The civilians, though injured, were able to do what they could to help them. Prescott soon headed off to the south, a lucky choice, and four miles later came across Tir y Cwm farm and raised the alarm. A search party was formed by Police Sergeant Thomas at Ystradgynlais, and they headed up the mountain slopes in dreadful weather. An all-night search on the trackless mountainside was fruitless. The Anson was not found until 6am next day. By that time, injuries and exposure had claimed the life of Aircraftsman Mabbott. Mr MacDonald was given first-aid and managed to make his way down with some help. It took five hours to transport F/O Coombes, carried in a parachute, to the road where he was speeded away to Swansea Hospital. Unfortunately he died of his injuries shortly afterwards.

A plaque was erected by the Southampton Training Aviation Company in Callwen Churchyard, Glyntawe, to the men of the village who risked their lives searching for one of their aircraft.

To the north of the National Park is Mynydd Eppynt, partly taken up by a military firing range. The high ground is a central ridge a little over 1,500 feet in elevation, running roughly south-west to north-east. It is well down on the lofty Brecon Beacons and so gave rise to few crashes.

South of the A465 road, the section between Abergavenny and Hirwaun, a series of valleys cuts through the high ground as the rivers head for the coast. Their names are renowned from the coal mining era. These hills also claimed a small share of aircraft. One of these involved de Havilland Vampire VV618, which took off from RAF Merryfield on 27 October 1953 on a cross-country exercise. Piloted by P/O D. V. Reypert, it flew to RAF Valley in Anglesey to refuel and took off again at 1550 hours. Some 30 minutes later it was seen to emerge from cloud above Rhymney, losing height. Suddenly, one of the external fuel drop tanks fell away and impaled itself on the vicarage railings, after which the aircraft made a steep climbing turn back up into the cloud. Soon afterwards it emerged from the cloud in a shallow dive and impacted the ground at the head of the valley at 1625 hours, killing the pilot.

Further north, and still moving west, the Black Mountain peters out before Ammanford and Llandeilo and we reach more undulating terrain before and after Carmarthen. Heading for the western view of Cardigan Bay, and thinking we are done with mountains, we are suddenly confronted by Mynydd Preseli – the Preseli Hills, their highest point Foel Cwm-cerwyn at 1,760 feet. The area has been inhabited for thousands of years, with an extensive trade in axes and other implements from the local rock. During the third millennium BC eighty huge stones of spotted dolerite weighing over 250 tons were hewn out of the bluestone area of Carn Menyn and transported to Salisbury Plain and Stonehenge. Historians and archaeologists would give their eyeteeth to travel back in time to see the process – and how did they move such weights across the Bristol Channel? The area abounds in legends. In one of these a huge wild boar, Twrch Trwyth, ravaged Ireland and crossed the Irish Sea to land at Porth Clais. It was followed by King Arthur who chased it over the Preseli Hills, losing many of his best men in the process. Eventually the boar was run to earth in Cornwall.

There have been seven aircraft crashes on the spine of these hills, including one civil, plus a Wellington a little to the west on Mynydd

Above: An Avro Anson at No.10 Radio School, Carew Cheriton. (*Hazel Nutter*)

Tre-newydd. The first incident occurred on 26 February 1940. A Fairey Battle, K7688, of No. 9 B&GS based at Penrhos, near Pwllheli, took off on a cross-country flight to Stormy Down. Entering a band of coastal thick mist, the pilot made a forced landing near the summit of Carn Bica, without injury to himself or his two companions.

One of the units based at RAF Carew Cheriton was No.10 RS (Radio School). On 15 December 1944, Anson EG639 took off on a radio training exercise with pilot F/Sgt Kenneth Owens and wireless operator Sgt John Venus. In poor visibility, the aircraft struck the ridge to the northeast of Foel Cwm-cerwyn, killing the crew. The wreck was not found for two days, so mistakenly the date on the headstones of the crew reads 17th. F/Sgt Owens, though born in Tredegar, was from Colne in Lancashire just twenty miles from where the Anson was built at the Avro factory at Yeadon.

One hopes that across the mountains of South Wales hikers will look at what is left of the crash sites, think of the airmen involved, and leave the pieces for posterity for those to come to see what sacrifices were made for them.

Chapter 2
A Miscellany of Breconshire Crashes

by W. J. L. (Len) Roberts

During World War 2, the air space of Wales was used extensively by the Royal Air Force, and particularly by its OTUs (Operational Training Units). Their task was to give airmen who had completed flying training some experience on the type of equipment and aircraft they would be using to fight the enemy. Bomber crews learned to fly as a team, the safety of the aircraft depending on the efficiency of every member of that team, hence the intensive training programme which continued in all kinds of weather. Much of the flying took place in the skies above Breconshire and inevitably a number of crashes occurred and many brave men met their end, mostly on our local mountains. This then is the story of just eight of the bomber crashes, no fewer than six of them being twin-engined Wellingtons. The other two were huge four-engined Lancasters.

The war was not three weeks old when the first of these incidents took place at Pont Nedd Fechan. On the evening of 18 September 1939, Wellington serial L4526 took off from Harwell near Didcot. It was piloted by F/Lt A. H. Smythe with F/O P. J. R. Kitchen as second pilot. They were engaged upon a cross-country navigational training exercise. During the course of the flight the weather took a turn very much for the worse, so when the wireless operator could not make contact with ground control, they realised that they were lost.

The pilot set the engine controls on their most economical setting, calculating to fly until first light when they hoped they would be able to see somewhere to put down. Dawn came around six-thirty and they were almost out of fuel. Below them all they could see were mountains. The order was given to abandon the aircraft and the crew took to their parachutes, all of them landing with no serious injury. A witness from Pont Nedd Fechan remembers seeing the airmen being brought into the police

Left: Wellington R1465 on Waun Rhyd.
(*Len Roberts*)

Below left: Wellington R1465 on Waun Rhyd.
(*Len Roberts*)

Bottom left: The crankshaft from an engine of
Lancaster W4929 on Fan Foel. (*Len Roberts*)

Right: Sergeant Walter Barr, survivor from
Wellington BJ697. (*Walter Barr*)

station in Glyn Neath, where they were given tea. The Wellington plunged
steeply into a small copse above the village, where a lot of wreckage remains
to this day but is mostly overgrown by tree roots and undergrowth. One of
the Pegasus engines is plain to see in a small crater, but needless to say is
rather bent.

Our next story begins at Marham near Downham Market in Norfolk,
the home of No.115 Squadron, at the time operating Wellingtons. Here
on the night of 8 December 1940, nine aircraft took off to attack a target
in Bordeaux, France. The weather was not good with heavy cloud, rain
and strong winds, but the target was successfully located and attacked.
On the return journey, the weather became even worse and the aircraft
became separated. One of the Wellingtons, serial T2520, made radio
contact with Tangmere and reported descending through thick cloud.
Tragically they were not descending over the flat lands of Norfolk, but
were coming down over the very rocky Cefn yr Ystrad, which lies just
north of Rhymney. At little after 3am on 9 December, the Wellington
struck the rocks close to the summit where it disintegrated and burst into
a fierce flaming mass. So intense was the heat that much of the metal
fused together. Signs of the conflagration can still be seen, and small
pieces of the plane remain amongst the rocks. The crew of six were killed

instantly. Three of them, P/O A. Tindall of Sydney, Australia, pilot; Sgt A. Brown, RNZAF, air gunner; and Sgt S. Howard, wireless operator, are buried at Llantwit Major Cemetery. The others were Sgt D. Mills, second pilot; Sgt H. D. Ellis, navigator; and Sgt D. E. Wallace, air gunner.

On 8 April 1942, Wellington R1597, pilot Sgt J. Kennedy, from No. 23 OTU was flying near the northern edge of the Eppynt range when it was struck by lightning and crashed on a mountain spur above Troed y Rhiw Farm on the outskirts of Llangammarch Wells. The crew of five perished where the aircraft struck the ground. Later in the year on the evening of 6 July, Wellington R1465 took off from No. 22 OTU at Wellesbourne Mountford, near Stratford-on-Avon. It was a former 214 Squadron aircraft that had seen active service with the unit before being downgraded to training duties. The crew were of Canadian origin and all sergeants. They were J. B. Kemp, pilot; E. E. Mittell, observer; K. F. Yull, bomb aimer; H. C. Beatty, wireless operator, and J. P. Hayes, air gunner. They, too, were going to fly a cross-country exercise. Flying in a westerly direction, they soon encountered heavy cloud formations, and it is thought they descended through thick cloud to try to pinpoint their position. In so doing

Below: The remains of Wellington MF509 on Carreg Goch. (*Len Roberts*)

Above: Lancaster Mk I W4333, 103 Squadron, photographed at Elsham Wolds in November 1942. Crashed 5 March 1943 by trainee Yugoslav pilot after engine fire.

they struck the top of the Waun Rhyd plateau and disintegrated in a high speed crash. An entry in the crash card states that pilots were advised not to come below 10,000 feet and it is difficult to understand why they chose to ignore this advice and descend to around 2,500 feet. The crew were killed outright and are buried in Hereford Cemetery. The wreckage of the aircraft has been collected together into two large piles and a memorial cairn erected at the spot. The engines have been pushed down the mountainside and one lies in the upper reaches of the Caerfanell, while the other engine is about three hundred yards away near the bottom of a steep gully which falls from the crash site. Children from a Tredegar school often placed flowers and poppies on the cairn and aircraft remains.

On the night of 25 September 1942, the landlady of the *Gwynne Arms* public house in Glyntawe saw a large fire burning on the mountainside to the right of the Haffes gorge. Her son and two guests who were staying there at the time went up the mountain to investigate. After a stiff climb, they could see an aircraft that was alight with bullets exploding from the fierce heat. Lying on the grass near the plane were the crew of five, four of whom were badly injured. The aircraft was Wellington BJ697, piloted by F/Sgt Bird who was the most seriously injured member of the crew. The other injured were Sgts Barr, Fairweather and Troughbridge, mostly with head and leg injuries. Sgt Head was uninjured and helped the three men to get his comrades down the mountain to the *Gwynne Arms*. The injured

Above: Vickers Wellington Mark 1c P9249. (*British Aerospace*)

airmen were taken to Neath hospital where the unfortunate F/Sgt Bird succumbed to his injuries. Sgt Walter Barr was brought down unconscious and taken to hospital where his parents found him after an urgent journey from Scotland. He was in other hospitals and convalescent homes, culminating with plastic facial surgery. Because of his injuries, he was invalided out of the service in March 1944.

Most of the wreckage was salvaged by No. 78 MU (Maintenance Unit) helped by local farmers using horses and carts. Numerous small pieces remain on the site amongst the rocks and under grass tufts. It is a difficult site to find and despite being located near the Brecon to Swansea road, it always gives an impression of being a very lonely spot.

The first of the two Lancasters was serial W4929. This particular aircraft had been on the strength of the famous 617 Dambuster Squadron, but was transferred before the raid took place. On the evening of 5 September 1943, it took off from Winthorpe, the pilot being Sgt N. T. Duxbury. The other crew members were P/O V. R. Folkerson, navigator; Sgt R. Wilson, bomb aimer; Sgt F. W. Pratt, wireless operator; Sgt L. Holding, flight engineer; Sgt J. G. Curran, mid-upper gunner; Sgt J. G. Buckby, air gunner; and P/O T. F. E. Johnson, an extra bomb aimer: a crew of eight in all. At around 11.30 a.m., the aircraft passed over the tiny hamlet of Llanddeusant and shortly afterwards struck the ground with great force just below the north-east ridge of Fan Foel. All crew lost their lives. An inquiry by the RAF into the cause of the accident was inconclusive because of the lack of evidence. From the state of the wreckage, of which a considerable amount still lies at the spot, it seems that the Lancaster struck the ground under power. Split propeller bosses, badly bent crankshafts and broken cylinder blocks of the Merlin engines certainly point to this and suggest that the crew thought they were flying over much lower ground, or else there was a fault with the altimeter reading.

The other Lancaster, JB471, crashed at 5pm on 10 April 1944 just outside Llanwrtyd Wells, near the road to Llangammarch Wells. The pilot lost control, possibly after entering cumulonimbus cloud, and the aircraft broke up in the air. One of the huge wheels was flung almost a quarter of a mile and just missed hitting farm workers. The plane burst into flames and a witness stated that members of the crew were trapped inside, unable to escape whilst onlookers could do nothing to help them. A truly horrific tragedy which must have played on the minds of the would-be rescuers ever since. The crew of the Lancaster were F/Lt J. L. Sloper DFC, pilot; Wing Commander J. D. Green, second pilot; W/O A. P. Malzan (Canadian) navigator; Sgt G. J. Shields (Canadian), navigator; Sgt H. Johnstone, wireless operator; Sgt S. J. Warrenger, flight engineer; Sgt J. H. Cleminson, mid-upper gunner; and Sgt W. W. Farmer, air gunner. Once again, a crew of eight.

Approximately two and a half kilometres to the north-west of Craig-y-Nos, there is a very rocky mountain by the name of Carreg Goch. It is a desolate area and exposed to westerly winds. A little

Right: W/O. Albert F. Malzan RCAF, back left, navigator of Lancaster JB471, and Sgt G. J. Shields holding a dog. It is possible that all these airmen were in the crew of Lancaster JB471. (*Alun Evans*)

way down its west slope falling to the Giedd lies the wreckage of Wellington MF509. There is a great deal of wreckage with much more lying amongst rocks to the west and north-west. There is so much wreckage that coming upon this plane in a mist, one could almost imagine that it is a very recent crash and not one that took place on the night of 20 November 1944. On that night the Wellington took off from Stratford airfield and set a course to the west. Trouble developed with the starboard Hercules engine and at the same time, it is believed, the aircraft began to ice up and lose height. With insufficient power available from the port engine it sank rapidly to earth, striking the rocky ground to the north-west of Carreg Goch. The aircraft was torn to pieces, leaving large sections along its path where it lies today. The Wellington burst into flames and all six crewmembers perished. They were Sgt C. Hamel, pilot; Sgt J. R. Villeneuve, navigator; Sgt J. P. E. Burke, wireless operator; P/O W. J. Allison, bomb aimer; Sgt A. J. Groulx, air gunner; and Sgt G. Dusablon, air gunner. All were Canadians and it is likely that they were buried at Blacon Cemetery, Chester.

A memorial plaque was placed on one of the oleo legs but sadly, and unbelievably, was stolen. Happily, it has been replaced with another plaque (courtesy of the apprentices at British Petroleum) which is firmly attached to a small stone cairn, and occasionally flowers are placed on this and the wreckage. It is heartwarming to see that people still care and that those fine young men have not been forgotten. 47 airmen crewed these eight aircraft and no fewer than 38 of them died. Only nine survived.

Chapter 3
USAAF Mishaps

During World War 2, some months after the Japanese attack on Pearl Harbor in December 1941, a steady stream of United States Army Air Force aircraft flew across the Atlantic to Britain. Airfields were hastily constructed across the flatlands of East Anglia for their bombers to wage a daylight war against the enemy. The RAF had decided early on to strike targets during the hours of darkness. The German defenders were to have little respite. The first obstacle for the crews who flew the Southern Overseas Route was the great distance between Natal in Brazil and Dakar in West Africa, two airfields often used that are around 2,000 miles apart. Some aircraft, held back by opposing winds, ditched within sight of the palm trees of the African coast.

Below: Crash site of B-17 Fortress 42-5903 on Pen Gwyllt Meirch. (*Len Roberts*)

Above: The crew of B-17 Fortress 42-5903 "Ascend Charlie". Back row L-R, S/Sgt P. Catania, S/Sgt Mason, Sgt. W. Hoffman, not aircrew and not on 42-5903: S/Sgt S. Rambo, S/Sgt J. Peterson, S/Sgt A. Manson. Front row L-R, 2nd Lt R. Schanen, navigator, 1/Lt H. Turner, pilot, 2/Lt F. Broers, co-pilot, 2/Lt O Tofte, bombardier. (*390th B.G. Museum via Derrie Edge*)

Another obstacle was running the gauntlet of enemy fighters, based in western France, after leaving Morocco. Some crews chose to fly further west, leading to the problem of locating their chosen airfield in Cornwall for refuelling before joining their squadrons in the east. Several missed Land's End altogether and collided with unexpected mountains in Wales. They had little topographical detail on their maps. This was a problem that also affected some US aircraft returning from missions, such as raids against the U-boat pens in western France. All USAAF losses in the area are included, high and low, details of which are not so easily found as for RAF aircraft but which in other works were appreciated by relatives.

A taste of what these airmen faced can be found in the pages of this volume.

THE BOMBERS

Boeing B-17F Fortress 42-29505
Unassigned. See Chapter 7.

Boeing B-17F Fortress 42-5903
571st Bomb Squadron, 390th Bomb Group

On 16 December 1943, this squadron based at Framlingham was detailed to attack the aircraft factory and airfield at Bordeaux. *Ascend Charlie*, piloted by 1/Lt Herbert I. Turner, was one of 21 aircraft that took off for the mission. They flew to Cornwall and made their approach from the Atlantic, to reduce the risk of being detected by radar or fighter patrols. When in the target area, the mission had to be abandoned because of heavy cloud. Targets of opportunity at La Rochelle were bombed instead. Here the formation was pounded by intense flak and *Ascend Charlie* was hit in its No.1 engine.

The aircraft of the group headed back over the Atlantic and turned for England. A radio message was then received warning crews that a weather front was approaching from the west. Hardly had the message been taken down than rain squalls hit them. These, and the onset of darkness, scattered the aircraft and each endeavoured to make it back to base individually. *Ascend Charlie* was seen by others in the squadron at 2017 hours, just before reaching the English coast. An hour later, at 2120 hours, it crashed on the summit of Pen Gwyllt Meirch in the Black Mountains, north-west of Abergavenny, killing all ten aboard.

Below: The crew of B-17 Fortress 42-5906 *Sondra Kay* taken 36 days before all except the navigator, Lt. William Eddy, top right, (not on flight) were killed. It was named after the baby daughter of S/Sgt Joshua M. Lewis, front row, third from left. (*USAF*)

Boeing B-17F Fortress 42-5906
567th Bomb Squadron, 388th Bomb Group

This Bomb Group with 21 aircraft had also been allocated to the same target on 16 September as 42-5903. *Sondra Kay* took off from its base at Knettishall, piloted by 1/Lt Henry C. Cox. It was one of sixteen that made it to Bordeaux like the 390th to find almost total cloud cover. Flying to the north, the submarine pens at La Pallice were located and the alternative target was bombed.

On their return they ran into the same adverse weather with one B-17 striking high ground near South Molton in Devon, killing two of the crew. Another found remote RAF Shobdon airfield on the Welsh borders at the last desperate moment and landed on three engines. The crew of *Sondra Kay* were not so lucky. They were seen off the English coast at 2037 hours, but some time later flew into high ground at Rhiw Gwraidd at Upper Cilge, Doldowlod near Rhayader, in bad visibility and with fuel running low. The entire crew of ten lost their lives. The aircraft was named after the baby daughter of S/Sgt Joshua M. Lewis, the tail gunner.

On Sunday 3 January 1943, some thirteen Liberators of the 44th Bomb Group at Shipdham, and Fortresses from other bomb groups, were to target the U-boat pens at St Nazaire. Eight B-24s reached the target and bombed it. On the return journey, Major Key, the leader of the B-24s, thought that the Fortresses were not on the correct course and decided to make for Pembrokeshire in the late afternoon without the necessary fuel to reach base. The crew of each aircraft searched desperately for a suitable landing ground.

Consolidated B-24D Liberator 41-23771
66th Bomb Squadron, 44th Bomb Group

With number 3 and 4 engines out of fuel, the first pilot, Lt Roy L. Hilliard and co-pilot, 2/Lt Dale Canfield, were forced to land without finding an airfield. The Liberator came down at a crossroads near New House Farm, Puncheston, near Haverfordwest, and disintegrated. The injured were removed to the War Memorial Hospital at Haverfordwest where 2/Lt Canfield of Chapman, Kansas, died that night.

Consolidated B-24D Liberator 41-23806
67 Bomb Squadron, 44th Bomb Group

The pilot of this aircraft was 1/Lt Roy B. Erwin and the co-pilot 2/Lt Clark E. Swanson. With both engines on the port wing out of fuel they attempted to land their B-24 nicknamed *Bat Outa Hell,* in a field. No. 3 engine failed as they came down and the aircraft dived from 600 feet into farmland at New House Farm, a different farm to the previous crash, at Dreenhill, near Haverfordwest. Both pilots and Lt Thomas G. Deavanport, the navigator, lost their lives. The rest of the crew, some badly injured, survived due to the skill of the surgeons and care of the nursing staff at the War Memorial Hospital.

Of the other 44th Bomb Group Liberators, 41-23808 headed for Templeton but was running out of fuel when the crew spotted the tiny Aberporth airfield. The aircraft was severely damaged in a landing attempt with its short runway totally unsuitable for large aircraft such as the Liberator. Its pilot, Lt Long, was highly praised for saving his crew from serious injury. Other bombers landed safely at airfields at Carew Cheriton, Pembrey, Talbenny and Templeton.

Consolidated B-24D Liberator 41-11591
721st Bomb Squadron, 450th Bomb Group

This aircraft was based at Manduria in Italy and was still sporting the codes of the 513th Bomb Squadron, its previous unit. On 29 March 1944, it left Casablanca in North Africa on a second leg to RAF St Mawgan in Cornwall. Its mission was to collect radar-bombing equipment and return to Italy. Due to fog, the Liberator was diverted to RAF Fairwood Common, near Swansea, but this airfield was also in the grip of fog. Since the Liberator was running out of fuel, pilot Harvey Helmberger ordered the five members of his crew to bale out. Four of them did at a height of only 500 feet and survived. However, the flight engineer, Sgt Walsh, refused to jump leaving Helmberger little choice but to get back into his seat and attempt a landing with the aircraft coming to rest in a hedgerow just off the airfield. Sgt Walsh had climbed into the co-pilot's seat but did not fasten his seatbelt and was thrown out through the windscreen on impact. He died three days later. The pilot survived.

Consolidated Vultee PB4Y Liberator 43-8753
US Navy Bombing Squadron VB110

This aircraft was a variation of the Liberator with a single huge tail fin

Right: B-26 Marauder 41-18252 *Mi Laine* at Macdill Field, Florida. Back, L-R, Major Berry (CO), Lt Reiss, Lt Reed, Lt Carby. Front L-R, Sgt Dusing, Sgt Fox, Sgt Shoemaker. (*Patrick Reiss*)

and rudder instead of twin fins. The type was used by the US Navy for anti-submarine and reconnaissance duties. On the evening of 24 August 1943, the aircraft took off from its base at Dunkeswell, near Honiton in Devon, on a route familiarisation exercise with a crew of six. Residents of Glyntawe heard an aircraft flying in a north-westerly direction towards the mountains.

The next day, wreckage of the Liberator was found at 1,800 feet on Moel Feity, one of the peaks of the Black Mountain. The crew, all of whom lost their lives were Lt (jg) John Glennon Byrnes, AV(N); Lt (jg) John Neill Hobson, AV(N); Ensign Andrew Manelski, AV(S); Hyman P. Holt Jr, AMM1c; Franklin R. Shipe, ARM2c; and Donald F. Keister, AMM3c.

The Martin B-26 Marauder was a formidable-looking chunky bomber powered by two enormous Pratt and Whitney 1850 horsepower, eighteen cylinder radial air-cooled engines. A formation of eight of these aircraft had safely traversed the Atlantic. To lighten their load, four of the usual five crew were carried and ammunition and some radio equipment was removed. On 4 June 1943, the formation took off from Port Lyautey, now known as Kenitra, in North Africa at 0700 hours in fine weather. Their destination was RAF St Eval in Cornwall. Playing safe, the crews chose to fly up the 12th meridian, well away from predators based in France.

Only the lead aircraft carried a radio set and radio operator, so the others had to remain in visual contact. That was the plan, but the British weather intervened. Clouds made an appearance and the aircraft became separated. Unknown to the crews, the wind had increased and pushed the bombers further north and towards the Irish Sea.

The lead aircraft, 41-34718, made a perfect landing on a remote beach near Drogheda in Eire. The crew, who suffered no injuries, were handed over to the British authorities in Northern Ireland soon afterwards. The Marauder had landed below the high water mark and was salvaged as scrap. As this was the only aircraft with a radio, what chance had the others? We do know that 41-34722 was able to land safely at Chivenor in Devon. 41-34738 somehow made it as far as Dalton in Yorkshire. Both aircraft suffered slight damage in landing, but all crewmembers were uninjured. Of the remaining five B-26s, we may assume that three landed safely. The other two crews ran out of luck.

Martin B-26B Marauder 41-18252
Unassigned

4 June 1943 found thick fog at Penrhyn Farm, at Pwll near Llanelli. Sixteen-year-old Hugh Bonnell was making his way to a corrugated-iron barn holding hay for the cattle. He was taking refuge from a heavy shower of rain in an outbuilding when he heard the engines of an aircraft flying south, away from the farm. Minutes later the aircraft returned but much lower. Hugh just made out the shape of the bomber flying at a height of under fifty feet and dived for cover into the outbuilding. There was a tremendous explosion. He dashed outside to find that the aircraft had just missed the farmhouse where his family were, hit a tree and smashed through the very hay barn where he was aiming for. He had been saved by the shower! The Marauder was unrecognisable, only smouldering pieces remained. The four airmen were killed. They were:

Pilot, Lt John Reiss from Corpus Christi, Texas.
Navigator, Lt Eugene Carby from Atlanta, Georgia.
Engineer, Sgt Raymond Shoemaker from Reading, Pennsylania.
Passenger, Lt William Shoop from Springdale, Pennsylvania.

Lt Shoop had joined the aircraft as a passenger after Major Erwin Berry, of the 449th Bomb Squadron, and part of the original crew of this aircraft, had injured his back falling off a wing of a B-26 at Ascension Island. Marauder 41-18252 had been named *Mi Laine* after Major Berry's wife.

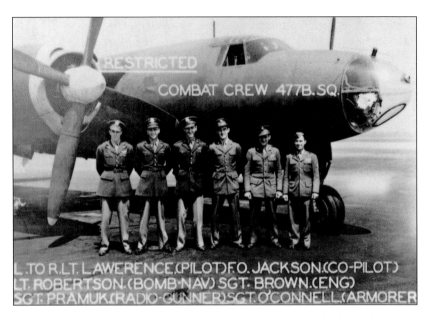

Above: B-26 Marauder 41-34765. The first four airmen, L-R, of this crew lost their lives in the crash on Carn Llidi. (*Gwen Scoggins*)

Below: The deadly outcrop of rock at Carn Llidi. The arrow shows the impact point of B-26 41-34765. (*Steve Jones*)

Above left: Lt Robert F. Lawrence, pilot of *Lil' Lass.* (*Barbara Tortenson*)

Above right: Lt Hulbert Robertson, co-pilot of *Lil' Lass.* (*Gwen Scoggins*)

Left: S/Sgt William A. Brown, engineer of *Lil' Lass.* (*Linda Keeler*)

Martin B-26C Marauder 41-34765

Unassigned

This aircraft was caught up in the same weather conditions and the crew must have descended to sea level in an effort to get below the fog. In these conditions the Marauder flew into the south-east face of the rocky outcrop on Carn Llidi Mountain near St David's, in Pembrokeshire, with the loss of the four young airmen. They were:

Pilot, Lt Robert Lawrence from Newark Valley, NY.

Navigator, Lt Hulbert Robertson from Comanche, Texas.

Engineer, Sgt William Brown from Havre, Montana.

Passenger, F/O James Jackson from Carrollton, Georgia.

On 4 June 2005, the 62nd anniversary of the crash, a dedication service was held at the memorial. Present were relatives and friends of the crew, Mr Brian Bolton of the US Embassy, Major Matt Goodrich (US Army), Councillor John George (Mayor of St David's) and over fifty local people. At 1615 hours, the time of the crash, a minute's silence was held to remember the four airmen who died on the mountain behind the memorial. The service was made even more poignant due to the presence of the daughters of Lts Lawrence and Robertson. The aircraft was named *Lil' Lass*

Above: The memorial service for the crew of B-26 Marauder 41-34765 held on the 62nd anniversary of the crash, 4 June 2005. L-R, Memorial service organiser Steve Jones, Major Matt Goodrich (US Army), Brian Bolton (US Embassy), Bobby Tortenson (Lt Lawrence's daughter, after whom the aircraft was named) Gwen Scoggins (Lt Robertson's daughter) and half-sister Alice Fulton, the Mayor of St David's Councillor John George, with Mayoress Nan George and crash historian Paul Cartwright. (*Steve Jones*)

Right: Ammunition from the A10 Thunderbolt. (*Len Roberts*)

after Lt Lawrence's older daughter, Barbara. The inquiry into these losses determined that all aircraft should carry radio sets and radio operators in the future, so crews did not find themselves in such a predicament.

THE TRANSPORTS

Douglas C-47A Dakota 42-24018
No. 77 Troop Carrier Squadron
   See Chapter 10.

THE FIGHTERS

Lockheed P-38J Lightning 42-67859
402nd Fighter Squadron, 370th Fighter Group
   This aircraft, based at Andover and flown by 1/Lt Coleman C. Richards, was on a cross-country low-altitude navigation flight on instruments to Aberdovey on 12 April 1944. At 1021 hours, it collided with a ridge of the Black Mountains above the Olchon Valley at almost 2,000 feet. The pilot lost his life.

Fairchild A10 Thunderbolt 80-0231
10th Tactical Fighter Wing, Alconbury
   On 6 February 1990, Capt Robert Burrowes was engaged on a low-flying exercise when his aircraft collided in cloud with a ridge of the Black Mountains to the west of the Vale of Ewyas, north of Capel-y-ffin. The pilot was killed.

Chapter 4

Night Raider Down

by Hugh Trivett

In the first week of September 1940, the Luftwaffe threw its bomber force against London in an attempt to draw RAF fighters into a final and conclusive air battle. To keep the pressure on the weary pilots – and to undermine civilian morale – night bombing was also intensified and on the night of 12/13 September nine Heinkel He111Ps of 8th Staffel, Kampfgeschwader 27, set off from their base at Rennes in north-west France. Flying solo or in pairs, they were briefed to carry out a series of nuisance raids against dockyards at Bristol, Plymouth, Merseyside, Swansea and Cardiff.

In He111P coded 1G+DS, Werke Nr 2670, Oberleutnant Harry Wappler took off at 2230 hours on a lone mission to attack the docks and

Below left: Unteroffizier Fritz Bernt on release from capture, June 1940. (*Hugh Trivett*)

Right: Oberleutnant Harry Wappler. (*Hugh Trivett*)

installations at Ellesmere Port. The journey was uneventful and, approaching the target, the crew leisurely went through the bomb release drill. Over the Mersey, there was a flicker of searchlights and the faint crump of anti-aircraft fire. The clouds gave the German bomber a cloak of invisibility and directly over the target a stick of bombs tumbled downwards. Mission completed, they turned south to unload their remaining 50kg bombs against their secondary target: the docks at Cardiff.

However, the weather continued to close in, and with very little radio navigation, they were forced to fly on instruments. Wappler continually asked for instructions from his navigator Unteroffizier Fritz Bernt, who equipped with only a watch and a compass, was desperately trying to plot their path southwards. Bernt had been shot down and captured during the Battle for France. He was released and returned to his squadron upon the fall of France.

There was still no visual contact with the ground and their apprehension grew with every passing second. After about five hours' flying time the navigator indicated that they should be over the target and Wappler took the aircraft down through dense clouds. At about 2,000 feet the overcast started to thin and approaching 1,000 feet they could make out the vague shapes of houses and the light from the firebox of a moving train. Following the wet and glistening railway tracks southwards they fired a flare to light up the area, and seeing the docks in the distance, commenced their bombing run.

After a quick supper break in the police canteen, 22-year-old PC Doug Cox returned to his beat near Newport town centre. A 'red alert' was in progress and to be on the safe side he had worn his .45 Webley pistol. This gave him some small comfort but on such a dismal night, and in the wartime

Above: KG 27 airmen at Wunsdorf, early May 1940. Oberfeldwebel Johannes (Yonny) Elster is fifth from the left. (*Hugh Trivett*)

blackout, it was a cold and lonely vigil. At about 3am, he found himself standing at the junction of Kingsway and Commercial Street when he heard the throbbing sound of an aircraft overhead. As the aircraft lost height the drone of its engines grew increasingly louder, and it seemed to Doug that the raider was heading straight for his position near the police telephone pillar. He immediately notified HQ of the situation and, not waiting for bombs to fall, rapidly made his way to the shelter in nearby George Street. Standing alone at the entrance he waited for the inevitable. Suddenly there was a bright red flash that lit up the western skyline followed by a terrific explosion. This was no bomb blast.

Levelling out the aircraft, Wappler closed in on what he believed was the dockland area of Cardiff when without warning the glazed forward section of the cockpit completely disintegrated. The Heinkel slewed right around a barrage balloon cable, and with a dull groan the starboard wing parted company with the fuselage. Wappler somehow managed to keep his hands and feet on the controls but the sudden rush of air and flying glass knocked him out of his seat. Momentarily suspended in the air he was deafened by the high-pitched scream from the engines, and a sharp, ever-increasing whine as the plane plunged out of control. Before he could shout a warning to his crew, Wappler was thrown clean through the shattered nosecone and out into the darkness.

He shot out and up and smashed against the tailplane, breaking his arm in three places, and almost passing out with the pain. Instinctively he pulled the parachute release with his undamaged left arm, and as the chute jerked open, he saw a bright orange flash as his aircraft exploded on impact. With his right arm hanging limply he had no control over the parachute and as it spun round ever faster he blacked out. At the controls of a Heinkel, the pilot sat in an all-in-one parachute suit, but because of their in-flight duties, such an outfit for the crew was impracticable. Instead they wore a harness onto which the parachute had to be clipped. From 1,000 feet, Wappler's crew had no chance to clip on their parachutes and bale out. The navigator, along with the flight engineer, Unteroffizier Herbert Okuneck and the radio operator, Oberfeldwebel Johannes 'Yonny' Elster, died instantly as the Heinkel crashed onto 32 Stow Park Avenue, Newport.

As it plunged to earth, the shattered Heinkel hit the top of 31 Stow Park Avenue and then exploded on impact as it ploughed into the lower half of number 32, the home of Mr Harold Phillips, a well-known Jewish businessman who was asleep with his wife in the front first floor bedroom. Their son Malcolm, aged 17, was in the room adjacent, but their 14-year-old daughter Myrtle had snuggled down in the dining room at the rear of the ground floor which was considered to be the safest place in the house. Within seconds, flames had engulfed the rear part of the house and the family was wide-awake with fear with the acrid smell of smoke in their nostrils. Malcolm rushed to warn his parents but they were already out of bed heading for the stairs. He shouted at them: "No! Go the other way!" in a brave attempt to rescue his sister, he turned back down the stairs into the raging inferno.

On his hands and knees, Mr Phillips tried to follow Malcolm but was beaten back by the thick smoke and intense heat, suffering burns to his hands and arms. Thinking quickly, his wife had knotted the bed sheets into a makeshift rope, and when her husband returned they lowered themselves to safety. Fuelled by a canister of incendiary bombs destined for Cardiff docks, the fire was raging furiously and as part of the floor collapsed, the rear wall caved in. Despite his injuries, Mr Phillips ran round to the rear of the house and smashed the library windows in a last, desperate attempt to save his children; however, he was beaten back by the searing heat and choking fumes. Finally restrained by a fireman, he was taken to hospital with his sobbing wife.

Right: PC Doug Cox. (*Hugh Trivett*)

Enemy at the Door

As PC Cox went to investigate the explosion, a sixth sense prompted him to turn into Queen Street, a quiet cul-de-sac off Cardiff Road. In the darkness his eyes focused on something white and luminous strung out across the road. As he switched on his torch he could make out the object was an open parachute fluttering faintly in the night air. Getting closer he could see it was attached to a lifeless, crumpled body in a green flying suit. Kneeling down he gently unzipped the suit to reveal a dark blue uniform, emblazoned with the insignia of a Luftwaffe officer. The removal of the bloodstained flying helmet uncovered a head of short fair hair, which to PC Cox was the archetype of a Teutonic German. By now it was obvious that his prisoner was very badly injured and, forgetting his initial prejudice, he tried to make the stricken airman as comfortable as possible. He then cut Wappler free from the parachute, took possession of his Mauser pistol and uncovered a gravity knife, which he slipped into his pocket as a souvenir. With some assistance, Cox managed to carry the wounded airman over to a nearby house and sat him down in an easy chair. By now, Wappler had started gradually to regain consciousness, muttering "Kameraden, Kameraden" and was offered a drink of water, which he declined. He seemed to understand what was going on around him but remained reticent to the questions that were put to him about his injuries. What he did say was rather incoherent and again he lapsed into semi-consciousness as other officers, under the command of Inspector Herbert Bliss, arrived with the military.

As his presence was no longer required, Cox set off alone to the scene of the crash at Stow Park Avenue. The road was littered with debris, but a Dunlop tyre attached to an undercarriage leg and an Ever Ready battery were clearly visible. The onset of war had obviously not deterred some manufacturers from dealing with the future enemy.

46

In the early morning light, Cox surveyed a sight of utter devastation. There was a faint flicker of flame from the gaunt, burnt-out shell of the house and one of the side walls had dangerously bellied out, making it extremely hazardous for the demolition squad. On the back lawn lay one wing, twisted and battered almost out of recognition, with its busted engine lying some distance away along the drive. The other wing had fallen in a shapeless mass across the avenue, with smaller pieces of wreckage landing on roofs and gardens nearby. The firemen soon recovered the bodies and the German airmen were buried without any formal ceremonies at St Woolos Cemetery, Newport. In the 1960s, the aircrew were exhumed and reburied in the German War Cemetery at Cannock Chase, near Stafford, Block 7, Graves 294, 295 and 296. Malcolm and Myrtle Phillips lie together in Jews Wood next to St Woolos Cemetery. Their headstone bears the poignant inscription: 'They were lovely and pleasant in their lives and in death they were not divided.'

Up, Up and Away

In the late afternoon of Sunday 23 November 1941, Harry Wappler, in the guise of F/Lt Harry Graven, and his companion, Lt Heinz (Hannibal) Schnabel, as P/O George David, slipped under the wire of the prisoner of war camp at Shaps Well in Penrith, Cumberland, and headed for the nearby railway line. Their intention was to steal a plane from the aerodrome that they had seen near Carlisle and fly to freedom. They had met and talked of stealing an aircraft when they were being treated for their wounds in the Royal Herbert Hospital at Woolwich. Schnabel had been a fighter pilot with 1/JG3. His Messerschmitt Bf109 was shot down near Aldington, Kent, on 3 September 1940.

After climbing aboard a goods train as it slowed down on a long upward gradient, they disembarked when it stopped at the southern outskirts of Carlisle at around 8pm. They audaciously walked straight through the town centre towards the 'drome. As they passed the camp entrance, a sentry shone a torch in their direction and shouted, "Who goes there?" Saying nothing, the Germans turned round slowly so the guard could see that they wore RAF uniforms. Giving a smart salute in reply, the guard watched as they continued their journey down the road. In the gloom, their disguises had fooled the guard, but would they able to do the same in daylight? Would their makeshift papers pass inspection?

Left: POWs at Gravenhurst, Canada. Lt Heinz (Hannibal) Schnabel, fourth left middle row. Lt Harry Wappler, sitting far right. (*Hugh Trivett*)

After spending the night hidden in bushes, they found a hole in a perimeter fence and walked unnoticed onto the tarmac. No one challenged them as they wandered around looking for a suitable plane. It was near midday when they finally came across a two-seat trainer parked by a hangar. They did not know it but RAF Kingston was the home of a flying training school. The Miles Magister R1967 they had spotted had been parked by Flying Instructor John Gibson on the taxi track for refuelling. When he returned from lunch he could not understand why it was missing. After making enquiries, a mechanic revealed that he had started the engine for two Polish airmen he thought were on a training course!

In fact, the mechanic had hardly given them a second glance as they climbed up into the seats of the aircraft. The controls seemed simple enough and the tanks were full, but Wappler knew he would need some assistance to fire up the engine. He called the mechanic over who obligingly swung the propeller until the engine caught and was running smoothly. They taxied over to the middle of the airfield, ignoring shouts from the mechanic to report before taking off. Turning the trainer into the wind, it was airborne with very little effort, and for Wappler it was a wonderful feeling to be airborne once again.

Setting a course for 170 degrees, they headed out at a height of 1,500 feet and soon passed over what must have been the Wash or the Humber. The absence of maps did not present a problem, but over the sea they had a moment of anxiety when three or four AA shells exploded in front of them. They ignored what they thought was a warning to turn back and continued their flight for German-occupied territory and safety.

After flying for about two to three hours, they were out to the east of Great Yarmouth with the shoreline now receding to a thin, dim line. Suddenly the engine began to cough and splutter, a sure sign they were running out of fuel – the Magister had a range of only 380 miles. Time was up. They guessed the Continent was at least thirty minutes' flying time away and, not wishing to take a bath in the icy-looking North Sea, they reluctantly turned west back to the British coast. Just making it over the shoreline, Wappler made a forced-landing at Caister on Sea.

A police sergeant was quickly on the scene and seemed to accept their story that they were Dutch pilots who had run out of fuel on their way to Croydon. Asking politely to see their papers, he accepted their temporary nature but was unsure how to proceed and telephoned his headquarters for instructions. He was told to get in touch with the nearest RAF base at Horsham regarding the refuelling of the aircraft. Horsham accepted the tale of lost Dutch pilots and sent a jeep to accommodate them for the night. It was already dark when they arrived at Horsham. After being asked some basic questions and being satisfied with their replies, they were shown to the officers' quarters. An hour later as Schnabel was taking a shower and Wappler was in the bathtub, they were confronted by the officer-in-charge and three attendant officers. Realising the game was up, they admitted that they were Luftwaffe POWs who had escaped.

As they were being escorted from the washroom, they passed through the officers' mess where the RAF officers had now gathered. Many wore cheerful grins and some gave the thumbs up sign and slapped their backs as they were led to the guardroom. Except for a number of soldiers who were present, everyone thought it was a huge joke. After a brief interrogation at Cockfosters, they were returned to Shap Wells where they were sentenced to 28 days' solitary confinement. Throughout this, they were continually asked about their means of escape, but they gave nothing away. They were both transported to Camp 20 at Gravenhurst in Canada, from which escape would prove much more difficult.

But not impossible! In his book *Full Circle*, Ulrich Steinhilper revealed that Heinz Schnabel, because of illness, was exchanged for an Allied POW via Sweden under the auspices of the International Medical Commission. Back in Germany, Schnabel wrote to the Steinhilper family advising them not to worry about any unfavourable news about their son, Ulrich, from Camp Gravenhurst. 'He is trying to reach home by pretending that he has a mental illness,' he wrote. This airman also succeeded in escaping, indeed once making it over the border into the US on a train before being caught and returned to Camp 20.

Chapter 5

Dornier Do 217 off Port Eynon

by Steve Jones

A spring tide and offshore winds are the ideal combination for beachcombing along the south coast of Wales. It was on such a day in April 1990 that I found myself sitting on a rock, waiting for the tide to recede to its full ebb. Spring had finally sprung; gone were the gale-force winds that had lashed Great Britain for almost the whole of March. I could feel the sun warming my back as I sat perched on the razor-sharp rocks off Port Eynon point. With only half an hour to go before low tide, I set off towards the water's edge to see what treasures the sea had exposed.

I had not walked far when I came across pieces of aluminium shining in the bright sunshine. I collected these pieces, examining them for any traces of identity. What were they off? A small boat perhaps that had been wrecked in the previous strong winds? An aircraft more likely. Had they come from an Air India jet which had crashed off Ireland? Parts of this aircraft had been washed up at Cefn Sidan beach, a large expanse of sand about fifteen miles west of Port Eynon. After collecting a good handful of these pieces from amongst the rock pools I started my journey back to the car park.

About twenty yards ahead, my eyes caught sight of another piece of aluminium. This particular piece had more of a shape to it than the previous pieces. On closer examination, I found that it was the barrel section of a double barrel flare pistol. A cartridge was still wedged in one of its barrels and had been fired. Also, at the stock end of the barrel, I noticed the emblem of an eagle stamped into the aluminium with the letters SP directly under the eagle's talons. This I had seen many times before in war films. It was the emblem of the German air force of World War 2 – the Luftwaffe.

Stories of a German aircraft crashing off Port Eynon point had

Above: A Dornier Do 217 at Schiphol airport. (*Steve Jones*)

circulated around local diving clubs for quite a few years. Various tales had emerged on how it came to be there, including the most common: "It was shot down by Spitfires." I thought it would be an interesting project to try and find out more about this mystery aircraft. Divers in general hold their cards close to their chest, so I found myself sweeping the seabed off Port Eynon with a metal detector whenever I could, hoping to find the main crash site. Calm sunny days would find me close to exhaustion at the water's edge, before the long walk back to the car. On emerging from the water on one such day I was confronted by a group of schoolchildren, curious to know if I had just swum over from the north Devon coast.

After several surveys of the seabed, I came across small parts with what appeared to be cooling fins still attached. They turned out to be pieces of cylinder head. This eliminated at least two of the more common types of Luftwaffe aircraft used against this country, namely the Heinkel He111 and the Junkers Ju88, which were both powered by liquid-cooled engines. The year 1992 dawned and I had still not found the main site. I located various parts of the aircraft, and little did I know that the aircraft's identity lay before my very eyes – but in coded form, stamped onto some of the components I had found. For a good example: R8 217. Knowing little about aircraft and their coding systems at that time I continued my search of the seabed.

On 22 June 1992, (the longest day of the year) I managed to persuade a good friend of mine to mind the boat while I went down to have a look at an unsearched area of the sea. Within the first five minutes of my dive my pulse rate doubled as two man-made objects rose on the sandy seafloor. At long last I had found the main crash site. As previously mentioned, they were air-cooled radial engines. Their cylinders had all been knocked off with the impact of the crash and lay close by, half buried in the sand. No propellers were evident on the front of the engines; they had probably suffered the same fate as the cylinders. Turning away from the engines I caught a glimpse of ammunition cases littering the seabed, a good way of dating the aircraft, I thought. Pushing my hands into the soft sand I pulled out handfuls of brass cases. As far as I was concerned they might as well have been gold coins. Later inspection found them to be 13mm rounds dated 1941.

Other wreckage lay nearby, some easily identifiable such as undercarriage legs. Others were totally unrecognisable due to the growth of marine creatures. I looked at my air gauge and, as always when finding something of interest under water, time had run out. Before leaving the site I managed to locate a small component with some numbers stamped on it which I had found near one of the engines. Tucking this part into my life jacket, I set off on my ascent to the surface. At this stage I was most concerned with getting to the surface to mark the spot with a buoy before the tide swept me too far away. As darkness approached I managed to get some good transit points. The journey back to shore found me reflecting on the two years it had taken me to find the aircraft.

The next day I cleaned the parts I had found, and on one particular part the numbers R9 801 were revealed. Reading books on aircraft components, I found that R8 which I mentioned earlier was the code for German airframes. R9 was the code for German engines. These letters and numbers were then followed by model or type identification, i.e. 217 related to the Dornier Do 217, thus R8 217, and 801 related to the BMW engine, thus R9 801.

On the night of 16 February 1943, Swansea suffered its last major air raid of the war. One of the raiders that night was Dornier Do 217 U5+FM, Werke Nr 5428. It was from 4 Staffel (squadron), Kampfgeschwader 2 (bomb group) based at Eindhoven in Holland. The crew consisted of:

Unteroffizier Günther Hübenthal, pilot
Unteroffizier Karl Hochmuth, wireless operator
Gefrieter Hans Krause, flight engineer
Obergefreiter Kurt Brand, observer

At around 2200 hours, the Dornier found its way over Swansea and was

Left: Unteroffizier
Gunther Hubenthal,
pilot of the Dornier.
(*Kurt Hubenthal via Steve Jones*)

Below left: Unteroffizier
Karl Hochmuth,
wireless operator of the Dornier.
(*Siegfried Hochmuth via Steve Jones*)

Above: Steve Jones with Kurt Hubenthal, pilot's brother. (*Steve Jones*)

Below: Steve Jones with Siegfried Hochmuth, wireless operator's brother. (*Steve Jones*)

intercepted by a Beaufighter of 125 Squadron based at Fairwood Common. Two pilots who were airborne that night claimed this Dornier as destroyed. F/Lt W. Jameson and P/O H. Newton both claimed in their combat reports to have shot down U5+FM into the sea. In the confusion of night aerial combat it is possible that both pilots contributed to the aircraft's fate. The fact is that the Dornier's port engine was set on fire and at 2225 hours the aircraft crashed into the sea in flames off Port Eynon, Gower. There were no survivors.

P/O Newton claimed two aircraft that night. Strangely, on landing back at base, it was revealed that Jameson's radar operator, P/O Crookes, had been shot in the leg during the combat and this turned out to be a .303 round – a British bullet! On close examination of the Beaufighter, an unexploded 20mm cannon round was found in one of the fuel tanks. P/O Newton was awarded the DFC for his actions and soon afterwards was posted from the squadron.

On 25 April 1943, the decomposed body of a German airman was washed up at Rhossili beach, five miles to the west of the crash site. It was that of Obergefreiter Kurt Brand. Initially buried at St Hilary's church, Kilby, his remains were re-interred at the Soldatenfriedhof, Cannock Chase, Staffordshire, in April 1963. The bodies of the other three crew-members were never found.

In January 2004, I placed a request for information about Gunther Hubenthal, the Dornier's pilot, in a newspaper which served his home town of Halle in eastern Germany. It took only a few days after the article was published for a journalist from the Saale Kurier newspaper to contact me with the news that Gunther had a brother who was still alive. Kurt Hubenthal, a retired opera singer, had often wondered of the circumstances surrounding his younger brother's loss. The only details the family was given were that he had failed to return from a mission over Britain, his eighth operational sortie.

After exchanging letters, painstakingly translated by his granddaughter Susann, I decided to pay him a visit. During my stay I was able to meet Siegfried Hochmuth, brother of Karl Hochmuth, the Dornier's wireless operator. Kurt's daughter, Maria, had been able to track him down from an old address on the back of a crew photograph, once belonging to Gunther. Apolda, the home town of Hans Krause, the Dornier's flight engineer, was only an hour's drive from Siegfried's home. Although we found no immediate family here, Maria had again done groundwork prior to my trip and contacted Marianne Althause, aged 92, a distant relative. She directed us to a former clothes shop, once owned by Hans Krause's father, Franz. His name was still above the shop front.

In the final hours of my stay with Kurt Hubenthal, he showed me his brother's ceremonial Luftwaffe dagger. In an emotionally charged few minutes, he kissed the dagger and presented it to me as a token of his appreciation for my research into his brother's aircraft – a very special moment.

Author's note: The last bombing raid on Swansea on 16 February 1943 was code-named *Operation Wasservogel* (Waterbird). 35 civilians were killed and 60 injured. At RAF Fairwood Common, the base of 125 (Newfoundland) Squadron which hunted the raiders, three WAAFs lost their lives: Patricia Baxter, Judy Chandler and Irene Collett.

Another raider, Dornier Do 217 from 5th Staffel, KG2, was U5+FN,

Werke Nr 5532. It was shot down by Wing Commander R. F. H. Clerke, commanding officer of 125 Sqn, and radar operator P/O D. H. Spurgeon. Hptmn H. Euler, Staffelkapitän, tried to land his damaged aircraft, but hit fruit trees and buildings at South Buckham Farm, Beaminster, Dorset. The crew of four were killed instantly.

Left: A propeller blade from Dornier U5+FM. (*Steve Jones*)

Below: A Beaufighter of 255 Squadron with radome nose housing the radar aerial, seen at Foggia. (*BAE Bristol*)

Chapter 6

Dowding's Dream

This is a story with a beginning and an ending, but with no middle. The middle is an abiding mystery. 'Tenacity' was the motto of No. 166 Squadron, in 1944 based at RAF Kirmington in Lincolnshire. It could also be said to relate to one of their airmen in particular. Airmen who had come together as bomber crews at the various Heavy Conversion Units went on to their designated squadrons for operational service. Here they undertook a few cross-country training flights before going operational.

One such flight was undertaken by Lancaster ND707, AS-E, which took off from Kirmington at 1430 hours on 9 December 1944 with a 21-year-old Canadian, P/O R. H. Chittim, at the controls. At 1610 hours, whilst flying at 24,500 feet over the Brecon Beacons, the aircraft flew into the centre of a huge cumulonimbus cloud. It was caught in a violent updraught which threw the Lancaster onto its back. When the aircraft righted itself, it went into a screaming dive, the members of the crew thrown about like puppets. In the confusion of half-shouted messages on the intercom and visions of their plane hitting the ground, four crewmembers baled out.

The pilot finally regained control, pulled out of the dive at 8,000 feet and headed for RAF Fairwood Common near Swansea where he made an emergency landing with the remaining two crewmen. One of these, the radio operator Sgt George A. Abrams, had been thrown across the main spar and sustained serious internal injuries. It is believed that he never flew again. The camp adjutant brought together a search party after hearing of the incident and set off for the Black Mountain. Three of the four parachutists had been found on the northern slopes of the Carmarthen Fans near to the village of Llanddeusant; however, there was no sign of the flight engineer, 19-year-old F/Sgt Trevor Charles Jones. His neatly folded parachute and flying helmet were found in the general area. He had vanished. (One presumes with early winter darkness that this was next morning.)

At 1630 hours on the 9th, the RAF Mountain Rescue Team at RAF Madley near Hereford, led by the station medical officer, S/Ldr J. Higginbottom, was alerted to stand by for a search. This followed a signal that four airmen had baled out over the Brecon Beacons. The team then travelled to Brynmawr and conducted a search of the mountains to the north. The news of the missing airman travelled fast and it reached the ears of Air Marshal Sir Hugh Dowding, the architect of our aerial defences during the Battle of Britain and an airman to whom a statue akin to Nelson's column might not be amiss, along with the names of the aircrew lost etched round the base. Dowding had a deep interest in spiritualism. A signal was received from him at RAF Madley describing the place where Jones might be found, as passed on to the Air Marshal by a medium. This had resulted in the Madley team starting their search in the Brynmawr area. It was not until the next day that they moved on to Glyntawe, the nearest village to the parachute find, and on up to the peaks, keeping away from the dangerous cliffs of Fan Hir.

The Air Ministry was so concerned that it involved the BBC, which broadcast an appeal on 11 December for any information on the missing airman. It was feared he might have suffered injury or loss of memory. Many were involved in the search: army, police, RAF and local people. There was no sign of F/Sgt Jones. The searches were carried out in appalling weather and gale-force winds, such as occurred in the winter of 2006/07. On the 16th, Sgt Hans Pick joined the Madley team, on loan from the 52nd Austrian Division and with plenty of experience in Alpine rescues. Even by 21 December, according to the RAF Madley team logbook, the searches continued with many people still involved and the area widened to include the uplands above Llanddeusant, Trecastle and Sennybridge. Where was F/Sgt Jones?

In the early morning of 24 December 1944, hill farmer Gwyn James went up to give his sheep flocks some feed on their winter quarters, the lower northern slopes of the Black Mountain. Later in the day, just prior to dusk, he returned to check on them. In the lane leading to Pentregronw Farm, abandoned for the war, he found the heartbreaking sight of F/Sgt Jones's body lying so close to being saved. He had a broken leg, presumably from parachuting but just as possible from traversing the rough terrain. The elbows of his flying suit were worn away with crawling. The questions then burst forth: how was he missed? This was no place for anyone in the winter, with only short daylight hours, bogs, mountain streams, rocks, heather moor and the most inclement weather. At night, due to the blackout, no light of any kind save the moon could be seen. It was a most lonely place. But, there were plenty of search parties on the hills. The weather, though, was an enemy, cutting down visibility to mere yards at times.

We may make a guess as to his route. To have gone north he may well have come down on the northern slopes sweeping down from Fan Brycheiniog. Any further west and he would have been funnelled down into the valley, which runs down from the upland lake

Right: F/Sgt Trevor Charles Jones, August 1944. (*Ivor and Edna Jones*)

Llyn y Fan Fach and onto the track to Llanddeusant. This was the area where the three other members of the crew landed. Over the fifteen days he could have crawled east past the source of the River Usk, then near the Roman Camp he would have cut across the road between Talsarn and Pont ar Hydfer. This is another mystery. Why not turn onto the road, east or west to salvation? The abiding question will always be: why did he not descend the mountain to one of the many villages below and to salvation – the natural thing to do?

We may assume that he could have been disorientated. This general area had been used for military exercises before D-Day, with abandoned vehicles, spent ammunition and even a Churchill tank left to the elements. This must have seemed very strange to Trevor Jones. While there was plenty of water about, he would have had only his emergency ration pack and may have found some animal fodder such as beet left out for sheep to sustain him. The last section would be over Fedw Fawr, but not dipping into the steep valley leading to the Afon Bran. And lastly, the struggle to the farm seen on the slopes, but unoccupied – a final rebuttal – Pentregronw.

The police were called from Llandovery and the airman was carried on a gate down to the little church at Myddfai. Here on Christmas Eve, the Reverend Emlyn Davies held a memorial service for F/Sgt Trevor Jones. The next day he was removed to Fairwood Common, and on to his hometown of Hucclecote near Gloucester for burial on 30 December at St Philip and St James' Parish Church.

Trevor Jones had been a pupil at King's School and a chorister in the cathedral choir. Also, he was a fine athlete. Had he not broken his leg, it might have been a very different outcome. Lancaster ND707 was repaired and flown back to Kirmington. The remaining crew and replacements were soon over Germany. As well as P/O Chittim, they included F/Sgt G. H. Pearson, bomb aimer; Sgt T. D. Tarlton, navigator; Sgt W. J. Morgan RCAF, airgunner; and Sgt J. C. Lillis RCAF, airgunner. The Lancaster and its crew failed to return from a raid on Lutzendorf in April 1945, just a month before the end of hostilities in Europe.

Many years later, due to the efforts of Ammanford aviation historian Alun Evans, a plaque dedicated to Sgt Trevor Charles Jones has been placed in St Michael's Church, Myddfai. Trevor's brother Ivor, with his wife Edna, was at the unveiling.

Part II

THE SURVIVORS

Chapter 7
Gunga Din's Last Stand

You may talk o' gin and beer
When you're quartered safe out 'ere,
An' you're sent to penny-fights an' Aldershot it;
But when it comes to slaughter
You will do your work on water,
An' you'll lick the bloomin' boots of 'im that's got it.
Now in Injia's sunny clime,
Where I used to spend my time
A-servin' of 'Er Majesty the Queen,
Of all them blackfaced crew
The finest man I knew
Was our regimental bhisti, Gunga Din.

Gunga Din – in the poem by Rudyard Kipling – was a water carrier to British troops in India in the nineteenth century. He gave his life as he took a bullet meant for a soldier. Hence the expression: 'You're a better man than I am, Gunga Din.' A film in 1938 used the same title.

Many years later, in 1943, an American pilot came to inspect his brand new B-17 Flying Fortress at its base in the USA. On the nose he found the inscription in bold letters *Gunga Din*. The airman was Lt Dinwiddie Fuhrmeister who accepted the nickname Din as his own.

On 6 March 1943, B-17F Fortress serial 42-29505 took off from West Palm Beach airfield, Florida. The crew of nine and a terrier mascot called Booger, flew to Marrakesh in Morocco via Brazil, Ascension Island, Monrovia and Dakar. Aircraft leaving for Britain had been flying north on the 10th meridian, but German fighters operating from French airfields had shot some down. The decision was taken to fly up the 12th meridian, 200

Left: Nose of B-17F Fortress 42-29505 *Gunga Din. (Din Fuhrmeister)*

miles further west. The destination airfield was St Eval in Cornwall.

At 2300 hours on 10 April 1943, the Fortress took off into a pitch-black night and headed north-west over the Atlantic Ocean. The gunners were wrapped in blankets and sleeping in the radio compartment. Lt Art Titus was busy navigating with Lt W. J. Smith (Smitty), the engineer, looking over his shoulder. Din and his co-pilot Lt Emil Rasmussen were keeping their eyes open for enemy aircraft.

Din: "After flying around 750 miles we entered the area of the Bay of Biscay, well protected by the Germans because of the submarine pens at St Nazaire. This is where we encountered the leading edge of the weather front supposed to be way farther north. At our altitude of 10,000 feet, we ran into clouds and the turbulence began. For nearly 300 miles we were tossed about, experiencing lightning and St. Elmo's fire from time to time. Art Titus could only use his magnetic compass for our headings and at this point our radio operator was not allowed to use his equipment because of security. About 9am there was a break in the clouds below us and we caught a glimpse of some islands and some land. 'That's the south west tip of Ireland,' Art said. 'Take up a course of 88 degrees.' Midway over St George's Channel, a long break in the clouds appeared. We let down to 1,000 feet flying eastwards until the clouds descended to the sea when we climbed to 6,000 feet. Meanwhile Sgt May, the radio operator, identified our aircraft and asked for a compass heading. The answer given was 268 degrees, (almost due west) which Art said was absolutely incorrect. He was the navigator. We continued east. We later learned the heading Sgt May got was a German transmission. Had we flown west and into the Atlantic we would have run out of fuel.

"Believing we were somewhere near our destination, we began flying a two-minute triangular pattern above the overcast, using our radio to call for landing instructions. We received no reply. The red light on the fuel indicators came on meaning we had no more than an hour of fuel left. I explained our options to the crew: bail out now or ride it down with me.

Left: Capt Dinwiddie Fuhrmeister (Lieutenant at time of crash). (*Din Fuhrmeister*)

Below: Lt William J. Smith, killed in *Gunga Din* crash. (*Din Fuhrmeister*)

Above: Re-formed crew at Thurleigh, Beds, with B-17F *Red Fury*, July 1943. Back, L-R: Lt Emil Rasmussen, Lt Art Titus, Lt Jerry Kostal, Capt Din Fuhrmeister. Front, L-R: S/Sgt George Toney, S/Sgt Ray Wilson, S/Sgt Owen Nabors, S/Sgt Chas Vondrachek. Not in photo are T/Sgt. Amos R. May, radio operator and T/Sgt Ode F. Harvey, engineer. (*Din Fuhrmeister*)

They all decided to ride. Art gave me a westerly heading thinking we would let down to the sea then try again to come again and land under the clouds or make a water landing.

"I think we're near mountains over Wales," said Art. With wheels up and half flaps, we descended 500 feet per minute at 120mph. At 1200 feet, Smitty screamed into the intercom, 'Pull up! Pull up!' Both Ras and I pulled the stick back with all our strength as we saw a black mass ahead... CRASH! It was a severe jolt. Then a bounce! We had lost all flight controls. Then crash again with a horrible grinding sound as the plane ploughed up the earth, scraping on the rocks and breaking apart. We had stopped!

"Then all was quiet except for the hissing of escaping oxygen from broken lines, rain and wind. Earth and dirt nearly filled our cockpit and acting impulsively we scrambled out of the cockpit windows. Fortunately there was no fire. Outside the aircraft now, and in shock, I counted noses. Except for Smitty, we were all present. Art told us that Smitty, as lookout, went out as if catapulted through the plexiglass nose on the first impact. We quickly assessed the situation, the damage to the plane and searched for Smitty. From the nose to the rear of the radio compartment was intact but the plane's skin was badly bent and severely damaged. The tail section was also quite some distance from the plane. Equipment, rubber life rafts, paper work of all sorts... and our personal belongings were scattered along the route for hundreds of feet!

"We saw scars at the edge of a 100 feet sheer rock face where we made initial impact. Not far from there we found Smitty in wet weeds, alive but unconscious and in truly bad shape. Collecting some blankets, we covered him and I soon cuddled him for warmth. Meanwhile, four airmen left to look for help, taking compass directions in fog and rain. We fashioned a stretcher out of metal tubing and blankets and got Smitty into the radio compartment to afford a little shelter from the elements. Art insisted we were in Wales, the only area with mountains so high. He was right!"

In fact the crash was on Foel Cwm-cerwyn – at 1,760 feet, the highest part of the Mynydd Preseli range of hills.

Din: "About 4pm we heard voices in the rainy foggy windy distance. Sgt Nabors appeared along with six RCAF groundcrew. They had been sent out to search for them when told of a missing aircraft in the area. Nabors met them coming up the mountain trail. They verified that we were in Wales not far from the ocean and Fishguard.

"Leaving two RCAF men as guards, the rest of us left the site carrying Smitty on the stretcher. Less than a mile down the mountain and out of the fog we arrived at their lorry which took us to Picton Castle, a British hospital near Haverfordwest. After giving us dinner, the doctor asked me to accompany him to the vault. There Smitty lay, dead. The doctor said many of his bones were badly broken and his insides lost their grip to his body from the terrific jolt he encountered when he was thrown out of the plane at 120mph. Sgt Keith Thousand was now in a body cast for his crushed vertebrae, Sgt Egbert's cheek was sewn up and Art's broken hand was bandaged and his arm in a sling.

"The next morning we awoke to a beautiful sunny day. Everything was such a bright green and this helped to make our memorial service for Smitty less sad. I believe his body was shipped home to his folks in New Jersey. Both Ras and I were black and blue on just one side of our bodies from the top of our heads to the tip of our toes. A nervous reaction was the cause, lasting around 48 hours. A lorry took Art, Ras, Sgt Wilson and me back to the mountain. When we arrived, the two guards were drunk. They had found our treasure of rum in the tail section and consumed quite a bit. They couldn't, or wouldn't, tell us where the rest of the bottles were.

"When we tried to reconstruct the accident, Art determined that we were 20 miles north of St Eval, our destination, and nearly on time when we encountered such a severe storm which then blew us way off course. It was a miraculous feat of navigation. We traced our path from impact to resting place and picked up what remained of our possessions. Ras and I determined that when we pulled back on the stick, we got the plane into a steep climbing attitude and literally pancaked onto the rocky ledge, causing the tail section to snap off. The plane then bounced into the air and, with no flight controls, met the earth at an angle and bounced again, digging into the earth before coming to rest.

"When we had seen all we wanted, we left the mountain emotionally drained after a final goodbye to *Gunga Din*, Smitty and Booger, our little terrier."

First Mission

In May 1943, the crewmembers, less Lt Smith and Sgt Thousand but with the addition of a new tail gunner, Sgt Harris D. Goldberg, entrained for the 306th Bomb Group at Thurleigh in Bedfordshire. Here they joined the

Above: S/Sgt Ray Wilson and wife Annis. (*Mrs Annis Knight via Steve Jones*)

367th Bomb Squadron, known as the 'Clay Pigeons' for their high loss rate. On 13 May, Lt Fuhrmeister would fly his first mission, as a co-pilot, for experience. This is his story:

"About 2.30am, the orderly awakened me saying, 'Wakey, wakey, lieutenant... The enemy awaits thee! Breakfast at 3, briefing at 4.' This is it! I'm going to war! My mind and body take on a variety of feelings and emotions as I shave, dress and say 'so long' to my sleepy officer crewmen who don't go today. As I pedalled my bike along the fog-dampened road, I felt uncomfortably excited. I was lonely without my crew and was joining a strange crew. I was afraid of the unknown. I asked myself why did I ever want to fly? Butterflies in my stomach were raising Cain. In a little prayer I asked God to get me safely through this day. We quietly ate our pancakes, heaven forbid, those gas-producing flapjacks. The higher we flew, the bigger those gas bubbles became. What a great relief it was to be able to fart!

"The briefing was held in a dimly lit auditorium at group HQ with benches for seating. Here I met my pilot for the day, Lt Onnen. I was to ride co-pilot to get the feeling of flying combat before going out with my own crew. The bombardier was Jerry Kostal, whose crew were shot down with a replacement. It was his first mission also. He would join my crew soon as bombardier. On the rear wall was a large movie screen, which when rolled up displayed a huge map of England and the Continent with coloured yarn marking the route to our primary target, secondary target and return route. The briefing officer announced to the officers and men, sitting there full of anxiety, 'Gentlemen, your target today is an aeroplane factory at MEAULTE, FRANCE.'

"There were some yeahs and applause which I interpreted as a target of a less dangerous mission. Yet, as the officer traced the route, he warned us of strong Luftwaffe defences in the vicinity and heavy flak over the coastal entry and over the target. British fighter escort could only take us 50 miles into France. We would be without them for 45 minutes. Our bombing altitude would be 28,000 feet.

"Jeeps took us to our dispersal area and our airplane fully loaded with bombs and 50-calibre ammunition. Her name was *Lady Margaret* No. 744. Lt Onnen gave us a short talk and told us to keep our eyes open and then we boarded the plane. We soon saw the single green flare from the control tower which meant we were to start engines. It was still dark. Then, a double green flare told us to begin taxiing around the perimeter and get into line for take-off. Now, in take-off position at the head of the runway, we checked the prop pitch, flaps, high rpm, the superchargers, the instruments – especially the artificial horizon – and satisfied ourselves that all was okay. We moved the throttles forward. On what seemed to be a long, long roll down the runway, the plane finally lazily lifted into the air. We were on our way, following by 30 seconds the plane before us, sighting his wing and tail lights for position reference. The predetermined compass and rate of climb took us to our assembly point over southern England.

"As dawn began to break, we took our position in the formation of 18 airplanes; 6 planes in the lead squadron, 6 in the low squadron and 6 in the upper squadron. I was to fly the plane until we reached the French coast, and after that, an observer. I thought it exciting to see the formations of British Spitfires flying above and on both sides of the bombers. Shortly after crossing the French coast, they left and the Luftwaffe became the 'escort'. High above us was a formation of eight Me109 fighters emitting vapour trails and flying into the sun where they disappeared. Then suddenly they dove, one by one from 10 o'clock high at our group. As they came closer, we saw 30-calibre tracer bullets streaking through the air in our direction. Tracers from our formation streaked towards the approaching fighters, the sound of our guns deafening and the vibration frightening. Then, as they came closer, the leading edge of their wings seemed to be on fire – caused by the firing of their 20mm cannons. A B-17 in the high squadron suddenly exploded. Then all was over for the moment.

"The shooting portion of the attack lasted only about ten seconds because the rate of closure was so fast. A few moments later, coming directly at us from the front and a little higher, was a single Fw190. It appeared to be dragging a bomb suspended on a long cable. The bomb dragged between the lead and high squadron doing no damage, but it was reported that the fighter was smoking as it disappeared to the rear.

"And then, flak! In front of us were thousands of black puffs of smoke from the thousands of artillery shells below which, when bursting, displayed a red flash. When shrapnel hit our plane it sounded like gravel being thrown on a tin roof. Aside from small holes in the skin of the airplane, the damage was slight. The group leader flew a zigzag course as evasive action to confuse the gunners below until reaching the IP (initial point). The lead airplane shot a Verey pistol flare as a signal to open bomb bay doors. For the next few minutes, we flew a straight and level course as the lead bombardier aimed his Norden bombsight at the marshalling yards and aerodrome, our target. The enemy fighters kept their distance because of the flak.

"Another flare and out dropped the bombs, with each of the 54 bombers doing the same. As we turned for our return trip, we could see the bombs exploding below, hundreds hitting the area. The targets were squarely hit! As we cleared the target area and flak, the fighters repeated their harassment, which they kept up until the British escort arrived. I saw some dogfights and destroyed aircraft, but couldn't tell which because of the distance.

"My brief remarks in my simple journal that night read 'First raid excited as hell. During the four and a half hours mission I felt we had seen a lot, and that the mission was more difficult than some had imagined. We had had a taste of war!'"

Dinwiddie Furhmeister survived his 25 missions into enemy airspace. His last foray took place on 30 January 1944; the target was Frankfurt in central Germany. As captain, he led the 40th Wing comprising some 800 Fortresses and Liberators, the largest USAAF force to date. They later learned that the Luftwaffe put up more than 700 fighters and some Stuka Ju87 dive bombers armed with rockets to combat the aerial armada. It was a battle royal. That evening, the German radio claimed 53 bombers shot down.

Din: "That evening I got on my bike and took a long, long ride by myself... and with God, I guess. I was terribly grateful for my safety and survival." Not all his crew were so fortunate. From time to time they would fill in vacancies in other aircraft. Ball-bearings used in every type of machine from tanks to aircraft were being produced at the town of Schweinfurt, 70 miles east of Frankfurt. An attack was made on 17 August when great damage was caused to the works there with small loss to the bomber force. The day came for the second Schweinfurt raid on 14 October 1943. This would be very different and known henceforth as 'Black Thursday'.

Sixty aircraft were lost. Lt Emil O. Rasmussen was flying as co-pilot with Lt Doug White when they were shot down. There were no survivors. Sgt George Toney was also killed. Sgt Amos May was flying with Lt Richard Butler when fighters shot out three engines of their Fortress. All the crew parachuted to safety and became POWs. Sgt Ray Y. Wilson, ball gunner, lost his life on 22 December 1943 on a mission to Osnabrück with another crew.

Left: Steve Jones with part of ball turret off *Gunga Din.* (*Steve Jones*)

Chapter 8

A Proctor Prang

RAF Madley, situated some five miles west of Hereford, was the home of No. 4 Radio School formed to train both ground staff and aircrew wireless operators. The aircraft used were de Havilland Dominies and Percival Proctors, installed with appropriate radio receivers and transmitters. Trainees started air instruction in groups in the Dominies, and then moved onto the smaller Proctors to practise individually.

LAC Frank Stokes was one of the latter. On Friday 12 January 1945, he took off at 1400 hours in Proctor NP216 on a routine training flight. The pilot was F/Lt E. P. Thomas, one of the few Nigerians in the RAF. He had 'bent' a few Spitfires in his earlier postings and it was rumoured that his father, a Nigerian prince, stumped up for a new machine each time! Frank Stokes recalls, "There was snow on the ground, but the runway was clear. Once airborne we were soon into clear air above the cloud layer. The operation was going according to plan when there was a change in light conditions. I believe the pilot had started descending. Then there was a lot of turbulence. Suddenly the drone of the engine changed to a roar, consistent with climbing as we tilted up. At this point everything happened very quickly.

"I could see the mountain ahead of us. At the same moment the port wing clipped a rocky outcrop. The aircraft slewed to the left and came to rest on what was a relatively snow covered grassy top. I was rendered unconscious and, on coming to, found I was still in my seat. My legs were cut when I must have hit the T1154 transmitter. My eyebrows and the bridge of my nose were cut where I had banged into the R1155 receiver. I did not have my lap seatbelt on because it was customary to loosen it when airborne (i.e. worn usually only on take off or landing).

Left: Sgt Frank Stokes, AC2 at time of the Proctor crash. (*Frank Stokes*)

"The pilot had been thrown forward and lay on the ground on his back. He was breathing heavily with blood oozing from his nose. He was several yards from me. I don't think he could have been unconscious for very long. As I stood up and looked around, all I could see was snow-covered high ground and no sign of civilisation (near the summit of 2,863 feet Corn Du).

"Thoughts of happier times passed through my mind. It was approaching 1500 hours and, as the country was on summer time all the year round, it would soon be getting dark. I would have to move fast or we both might perish. I first attended to the pilot by turning him off his back so that he was lying with his head down to keep the air passages clear. I was going to wrap him in my parachute but as I pulled the ripcord, the canopy quickly filled and the strong wind at this altitude carried it away. My next thought was to warm him up with the aircraft landing lights. This proved difficult as I had no screwdriver and a coin would not free the screws. I decided that I could hang about no longer, so set off down the mountain.

"I chose a path which was fortunately not too steep, and describing something of an arc as I cut across and down the mountain. It was bitterly cold and there was a gale of wind blowing. In places I sloshed through icy mountain streams until suddenly I caught sight of a road below me. On reaching the tarmac I spied a building up the hill, and struggled towards it. I found it was the Storey Arms Hostel and told the man inside my tale, which he passed onto the police by telephone."

Although a car was stopped to take Frank Stokes to hospital, he would not be moved until a rescue party arrived and he was able to give the members directions to the crash site. Then he allowed himself to be taken to Merthyr Tydfil General Hospital to warmth, safety and medical

Above: Fine study of Corn Du, where Proctor NP216 crashed. (*Brecon Beacons National Park Service*)

attention. In spite of his best efforts his pilot, P/O Thomas, died before he could be given the same treatment.

"My stay in Merthyr Tydfil was an experience I would not have missed. St Luke's Ward at the hospital was given over to the military. It was run by the matron as normal and there was no military discipline and no officers or NCOs in charge. The patients were mainly Welshmen who had been returned home after being wounded, some quite severely, in Burma. They had fought the Japanese in the jungles with some considerable success, mainly through speaking Welsh! The Japanese were keen listeners, with lookouts often getting quite close to our lines, but they just could not understand what they heard.

Some of the hospital inmates were within short distances of their wives, whom they had not seen for many months, or even years. This was not a problem for long. As soon as matron bedded the men down after supper and said her goodnight, the able ones were out of bed like a shot. They nipped out of the back entrance, up a convenient ladder and over the wall, but were back in their places, all smiling, by next morning. These men of South Wales would take me to their homes where I was shown generous hospitality within the limited means of wartime rationing and poverty in the area. Above all, their sense of humour came through, as would their love of music. I recall that in the ward, awaiting matron's morning inspection, there would be a spontaneous singing of a Welsh song or hymn. They were the salt of the earth."

During this time, Stokes received a letter from Newcastle University. It was from P/O Thomas's sister who was a student there. She wished Frank a speedy recovery and asked him for any details he was able to give and if her brother had said anything after the crash. Frank Stokes did make a good recovery although it was delayed by a compression injury to his vertebrae. Eventually he returned to RAF Madley and completed his course in July 1945, probably the last there before the station closed for flying. He was given his sergeant's stripes and WOP/AG brevet – as the war in Europe was over, he did not fly in the RAF again. A meeting with a Welsh mountain in cloud probably saved his life given the losses in Bomber Command.

In the light of his actions after the crash, Frank Stokes was commended for his distinguished conduct by Air Marshal J. R. Cassidy CBE, Commanding No. 27 Group.

Chapter 9
A Tale of Two Halibags

long with the Lancaster and Stirling, the Handley Page Halifax, affectionately known as the Halibag, was a stalwart four-engined aircraft of Bomber Command. Following problems with the rudder design of the Mark I, which could result in a loss of control of the aircraft, the Mark III with Hercules engines became the best design. Apart from its bomb-carrying capacity, in which role the Lancaster was superior, the two aircraft had a similar performance. Two accidents involving Halifaxes follow, one in the day and one at night.

The Day Job

Sgt E. L. Berry, known as Idris to his friends, had a wartime career punctuated with incidents. While at 19 OTU at RAF Kinloss, he was pilot of a Whitley that was showing lack of hydraulic brake pressure as he came in to land. As he approached the runway, a red Aldis lamp warned them off. The pilot opened the throttles to go round the circuit again, but the port engine failed. As the satellite airfield of Forres was straight ahead, a landing was made there. The Whitley, without brakes, landed on grass, ran off the airfield and across a road, and ended up in a deep ditch. The crew, thankfully, were unscathed.

On 22 August 1942, Halifax Mk II serial W1238 took off from Pocklington in Yorkshire, the home of 102 Squadron. Idris Berry recalls, "We were on a training flight, the purpose of which was the training of navigators in the use of 'GEE' (a type of radar which could be used for accurate position-finding over the nearer part of the Continent). There were three navigators on board: P/O J. M. Colquhoun, W/O C. E. Sorsdahl and Sgt S. Cooper. The other crew were Sgt W. E. Pattison, flight engineer; Sgt R. Hubbard, wireless operator; Sgt R. J. Horton, air gunner; and P/O Dale, a flying control officer along for the ride.

"The route was Pocklington, Reading, Fishguard, Isle of Man and Pocklington. On the second leg, at about 6,000 feet, the port outer engine failed. I immediately tried to feather the propeller without success. Consequently the propeller windmilled at 3,000 revs per minute, resulting in considerable drag. I was unable to counteract this by use of the port engine and throttling back the starboard engines. I soon realised that it was impossible to fly the aircraft on a straight path and maintain height. Whilst flying in circles and losing height, we were being dragged over Builth Wells.

Rather than let the aircraft fall on the town, I decided to crash-land on the outskirts. I told the crew that they could bale out or stay in the rest position. In the event no one baled out. In the last moments Bill Pattison moved over and strapped me in, otherwise I would have gone through the windscreen. The engineer just had time to hang onto the door leading to the rest position.

"After we touched down, the aircraft went through a hedge which ripped out the two front guns and made a large hole in the side. Eventually the Halifax came

Left: Halifax crew, not all on W1238. Back, L-R: Sgt Pattison, flight engineer, P/O Hargreaves, navigator, Sgt I. Berry, pilot, Sgt B. Wood, bomb aimer. Kneeling: Sgt Grimes, Sgt Foreman, air gunners. Dick Hubbard, wireless operator (*Idris Berry*)

Right: Sgt Reg Horton. (*Idris Berry*)

to rest, with the starboard wing up against a tree and the rear turret over the River Wye. The port outer engine was about 30 yards away, having been torn from its mountings. There was a fire inside the aircraft and the port inner engine also caught fire. Bill Pattison, the engineer, put out both fires and in doing so burnt his hand slightly. Otherwise there were no casualties. As we were approaching the field, I couldn't see a single person, but by the time we landed there seemed to be hundreds of people running down the hillsides towards us. Afterwards, the police told me that they had caught several small boys running away with belts of ammunition which had fallen out of the front turret." The forced landing took place on a field belonging to Mr Rowland Price of Gellycadywyn Farm, two miles north-west of Builth Wells.

The three navigators on that flight had varying fortunes afterwards. P/O J. M. Colquhoun RCAF was promoted to flying officer and was flying in Halifax W7918 DY-T, which was shot down on 27 January 1943 in an attack on Düsseldorf. The aircraft crashed in the Waddensee and he was taken prisoner of war. Colquhoun returned to Canada after the hostilities. W/O. C. E. Sorsdahl was awarded the DFM and survived operations to live in Calgary. Sgt S. Cooper was flying in Halifax W1055 DY-F, captained by Sgt R. C. Bassom on 23 September 1942. The aircraft was shot down into the North Sea while attacking Flensburg and Sgt Cooper was reported as missing.

On 24 October 1942, Sgt Berry flew a Halifax to bomb a target in northern Italy. On his return he found the airfield at Pocklington fogbound and was diverted to Holme on Spalding Moor. On arriving there he found that airfield also fogbound but, as the aircraft was almost out of fuel, had to land. Halfway along the runway, they hit a Halifax, which was stuck at an intersection with a burst tyre. Their starboard wing collided with the cabin of the stationary Halifax with the result that the squadron commander acting as co-pilot was killed and the wireless operator died from his injuries.

Above: Halifax Mk III emerging from the production line at Speke, about to be flown by chief test pilot John Palmer (in white suit). (*John Palmer*)

By the time Idris Berry was detailed for his second tour of operations in December 1944, he was flying Mosquitos with F/O Bolender, a Canadian, as navigator. On 2 May 1945, they were crossing the Dutch coast for an attack on Kiel when they both shot out of their seats as a V2 rocket just missed them!

The Night Job

One of the airmen posted to 51 Squadron at Snaith in 1944 was pilot Sgt A. S. (Bob) Jones. He had completed operational training and a conversion course onto four-engined Halifaxes with his crew. At Snaith, the squadron was flying the latest Mk III version with Hercules engines. Bob Jones recalls, "On arrival, we were given a short flight with an experienced pilot and were shown all the latest equipment and controls. After an hour or two of local flying, new crews prepared for a cross-country exercise before starting operations. On Sunday 21 May 1944, we made a

Right: F/O A. S. (Bob) Jones DFC, Sgt at the time of the crash of Halifax LK835. (*Bob Jones*)

45-minute flight and were briefed for a night cross-country flight to take off at 2145 hours.

"The weather forecast for the night of 21/22 May was good with a little cloud at various levels and, after taking off from Snaith in Halifax LK835, we climbed through some cloud to 20,000 feet and set course for a turning point in Scotland. The rest of our crew were navigator Sgt D. Bibby, bomb aimer F/O G. Cowd, wireless operator Sgt E. W. Luff, flight engineer J. Brown, mid-upper gunner Sgt T. Minns and rear gunner A. Westbrook.

"Our next course took us down the Irish Sea to Fishguard. Here we altered course and headed east for Cambridge. Shortly after turning onto this heading the flight engineer noted that the revolution counter on the starboard inner engine was flickering back to zero. I moved the pitch lever to check and the engine seemed to respond with a rise and fall in revs. Shortly after this the cylinder head temperature started to rise with the oil pressure falling. The flight engineer then advised me to feather the engine. This was not a problem since the Halifax Mk III was quite capable of flying on three engines with some slight adjustments to trim. To feather a propeller the pilot presses the feathering button and then closes the throttle. In this case, after pressing the feathering button for the starboard inner, it began to slow down but went into fully fine pitch and raced out of control. Sgt Brown turned off the fuel and ignition but this had no effect and a fire had started in the engine.

"At this stage I ordered the crew to stand by to abandon the aircraft. Parachute packs were clipped to harnesses and the crew acknowledged the warning. The engine fire showed no sign of dying out after diving the aircraft, and the decision was made to abandon since an engine out of control and on fire would have caused damage to the wing and loss of control. By this time

Left: F/O A. S. Jones; Sgt E. W. Luff, wireless operator; F/O Geoff Cowd, bomb aimer. *(Bob Jones)*

we had lost considerable height in all the excitement and were down to 7,000 feet. With the aircraft flying straight and level I gave the order to jump! The navigator released the hatch cover in the floor of the nose compartment and five of the crew left through this exit. The rear gunner left through the opening exposed by rotating his turret through 90 degrees.

"When I was satisfied that all the crew had left, I trimmed the aircraft and engaged the autopilot to fly straight and level. As I stepped down from the cockpit I still had thoughts as to whether the fire would go out, but decided to leave through the parachute hatch. The drill was to sit on the edge of the hatch facing aft and push off into the slipstream towards the rear of the aircraft. In these situations though, one always forgets the exact drill and I sat on the hatch facing forwards. As soon as I put my legs out, my flying boots shot off and were never seen again, but I managed to push off into the darkness. The time was 0010 hours on 22 May 1944.

"A sharp pull on the parachute release pushed the canopy out and stopped my fall. Everything seemed so quiet after the deafening noise in the aircraft. In a short time I seemed to be getting near to the ground, but it was very dark and difficult to judge height. This was probably just as well because I hit the ground without bracing my body. I did not appear to be injured and in no time some local people came to help having seen the burning aircraft and the crash. The Halifax crashed on fire into a peat bog at Waen Afon, in front of the old Milfraen Colliery, halfway between the tip and the road.

"A civil defence worker with the police went up with Sgt Jack Davies of the Blaina police and found two crew members on the Blaenavon road. Three other crew landed at Nantyglow and two at Blaina. We were relieved to find that all seven crew had made a successful jump and were now safe at Blaina police station. Later in the night, transport arrived and we were taken to RAF Madley near Hereford. After a check-up in the morning an RAF Anson took us back to Snaith where we completed reports and went through the previous night's events with the engineering officer. The investigation showed that the probable cause of the fire was a fault in the feathering mechanism followed by an oil leak onto an engine in fully fine pitch. We were all flying again four days later and started our operational tour on 2 June 1944 with a bombing trip to a German radio monitoring station at Ferme D'urville in the invasion area to come on the 6 June."

Soon after the crash, the crew became members of the Caterpillar Club and received gold caterpillar pins. Leslie Irvin's personal view of this exclusive club was that it should be membership for life; no membership fees; no joining fees; no official clubroom or hierarchy; only the common bond of having saved one's life by using an Irvin parachute.

Above: Halifax LK835 swallowed by a peat bog at Waen Afon. (*Len Roberts*)

Chapter 10

Finished by Fog

Many aircraft of the USAAF crossed the Atlantic to join the 8th Air Force in Britain. One such group in late October 1943 was No. 77 Troop Carrier Squadron, flying from Morrison Field in Florida via intermediary refuelling stops to Marrakesh in Morocco. Then the individual aircraft, C-47A Dakotas, set course for RAF St Mawgan in Cornwall.

One of these, serial 42-24018, took off from Marrakesh in the early hours of 5 November. The pilot was Lt Richard J. Burr, co-pilot 2/Lt George B. Callicoatte, navigator 2/Lt James A. Sigl, radio operator F/Sgt Harry Z Dow and flight engineer F/Sgt Charles W. Spencer. There were three NCO airmen passengers.

One hour from their destination the radio operator tried to make contact but, because of other aircraft being dealt with, was unable to get through. As time went on, the pilot decided to drop down to 600 feet while they were over water. As they were unsure of their position, they climbed through thick cloud to 4,000 feet and started homing onto RAF Valley in Anglesey. S/Sgt Dow then managed to contact RAF St Eval, another airfield in Cornwall, and obtained a QDM or bearing to fly, and made a 180-degree turn to the south. What the crew did not know was that they were over Cardigan Bay and not the Bristol Channel, so the south-west area of Wales was between them and safety.

The operator at St Eval advised that the cloud base was 800 feet, so the pilot descended to 600 feet as they came in over the coast. After some two minutes they were into dark cloud and started climbing again. All at once the pilots saw rising ground only thirty feet below them and Lt Burr started a sudden pull-up. A few moments later the Dakota hit the ground at 78mph. They skidded some 25 yards up a slope at around 35-40

Above: C-47 Dakota 42-24018 on Foel Feddau. (*Mrs Jennie Howells*)

degrees. They had crashed high on Foel Feddau at around 1,100 feet in the Preseli Hills. Unfortunately, as the plane hit the hillside, both propellers broke loose, port blades ripping into the cockpit and killing Lt Burr outright. The visibility according to the co-pilot was 25 yards.

The pilot had 975 flying hours to his credit, was very competent, and held in the highest regard by the entire squadron. No blame was placed on him for the crash. The accident took place at 1015 hours. At 1135, the radio operator was eventually able to advise St Mawgan of the crash, having been told by locals who arrived that they were in south Wales. Due to the remoteness of the site, it was some time before official help arrived. Aside from the pilot, the rest of the crew and passengers suffered only minor injuries. Some were later found hiding in the heather – they had heard Welsh voices in the mist and, thinking they were on the Continent, hid away!

Mrs Jennie Howells has lived all her life in the area. Here are her recollections of the event:

"My memory of the morning of 5 November 1943 – it was a morning of thick low fog. At around 1015 together with my father, John Rees, I was working on the farmyard at Penanty Farm, Brynberian, Pembrokeshire. Penanty Farm is on the Preseli Mountain. We heard the roar of a low-flying aircraft, and within a few seconds a loud crash. As a born shepherd on the Preseli Mountain, my father had a good idea of where the crash had taken place on Foel Feddau and he immediately left for the hill. When he got to the crashed plane, he met two survivors who, rather than talk to him, walked away. They must have been in shock.

"At first glance the plane looked as if it had come down intact. Later we heard that a loose propeller blade had killed the pilot. While my father was there, people from the village of Brynberian started arriving. So did our family doctor, Dr Milton Davies of Newport, Pembrokeshire. I can't recall how the survivors were brought down the hill. I believe that they would have been able to walk down.

"Personnel from RAF Haverfordwest took over to guard the plane and also to salvage it. We put the guards up at our farm, Penanty, for around three weeks while the salvage took place. My late brother Tom Rees of Penanty and the late Gwilym Rees Hendre Grosswell volunteered to bring the parts down to Brynberian. They could only use tractors to get near to where the plane had crashed. It was only by pulling the salvage parts behind the tractors that they were able to bring them from the hill to where a lorry from RAF St Athan was parked to take the wreckage away. Hardly anything was left on Foel Feddau where it had crashed.

"When the plane crashed it was a month from my 21st birthday. Though the young RAF men had left Penanty, they remembered my birthday with cards, letters and the photo of the crashed Douglas Transport plane on Foel Feddau, Preseli Mountain, Pembrokeshire."

1/Lt Richard J. Burr was buried at Madingley US Military Cemetery near Cambridge.

Right: George B. Callicoatte, co-pilot of the C-47 Dakota, on graduation from flying school at Ellington. (*Don Konley*)

Below: Foel Feddau in the Mynydd Preseli range, crash site of the C-47 Dakota. (*Mrs Jennie Howells*)

Chapter 11

A Whitley for Rhymney Hill

W
hile studying at Oxford University in 1937, Peter W. F. Landale joined the Oxford University Air Squadron and became a member of the RAFVR, so was soon called up when World War 2 began. F/O Peter W. F. Landale joined 10 Squadron at RAF Dishforth in Yorkshire in the summer of 1940, as a pilot for the twin-engined Whitley bomber. At first, he flew as second pilot to such airmen as F/O Henry. In September, now a flying officer, he became an aircraft captain, flying Whitley P457 on the 14th on an operation to attack targets at Antwerp. On the night of 12/13 November 1940, he commanded a crew consisting of Sgt P. D. Goldsmith as second pilot, P/O F. R. Goddard as observer, Sgt G. Christie as wireless operator and, way back in the rear turret, air gunner Sgt E. P. Lewis.

Along with the other crews, they were briefed to attack U-boat pens at Lorient in France in Whitley Mark 5, T4232 ZA-W. At this time, they were based at RAF Leeming, some miles to the north-west of Dishforth. The weather conditions were poor, with icing, which forced the pilot to reduce altitude. They also drifted westwards. In the darkness at 0142 hours, the aircraft suddenly struck the summit of Rhymney Hill near Tredegar. The peak is covered in rocks, which tore the Whitley's undercarriage off and caused damage to one engine. The crippled aircraft then dived down the mountain slope and crashed by a pond.

Fire broke out, a serious affair in an aircraft loaded with high-explosive bombs and incendiaries. All of the crew were badly injured, with the second pilot knocked unconscious. Sgt Christie left the wireless operator's position and, thinking they had come down on water, threw the dinghy out. He then proceeded to evacuate his comrades one by one, placing them out of reach of the exploding ammunition.

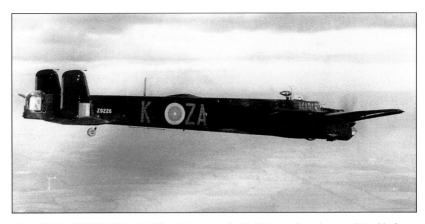

Above: Whitley V Z9226, K-ZA of 10 Sqn. It later served with 77 Sqn and was lost over Düsseldorf on 28 December 1941. (*Simon Parry/Red Kite*)

Sighting a farm building in the gloom, Sgt Christie then made his way there. It was Pen Bryn Oer, owned by Mr Hawthorne. On hearing the crash he had thought it to be a German bomber. He and his son went back to where the badly injured crewmembers were and took them into a room in the farm. Then the farmer got out his van and, with the aid of his son and Sgt Christie, carefully lifted the airmen and took them to Rhymney Cottage Hospital. Here they were attended to by Dr Leaun Evans. Sadly, the second pilot, Sgt Peter Dickens Goldsmith RAFVR, died because of severe internal injuries. The others recovered over the weeks but F/O Landale was in hospital for six months before returning to duty. In the meantime, he had been awarded the Distinguished Flying Cross for his great courage and skill, and for setting a very high standard of airmanship in the squadron.

Not so long after resuming flying and after further promotion on 25 July 1941, F/O Landale and F/Sgt Christie with three others in their crew were briefed to make an attack on a target at Hanover. Their Whitley was shot down and all the crew lost their lives. S/Ldr Peter Wellwood Fortune Landale of Dumfries has no grave but his name is commemorated on the Air Forces Memorial at Runnymede, panel 28. F/Sgt George Christie of Aberdeen is buried in Kiel War Cemetery, Plot 3, RQW B, grave 2.

Temporary W/O Ernest Philip Lewis was aboard Whitley P5016 of 10 Squadron which went missing on an operation to attack Bremen on the night of 27/28 June 1941. The other members of the crew were Sgt D. P.

Above: Peter W. F. Candale, pilot of Whitley T4252, seen here with the Oxford University Air Squadron in 1937, middle row, 7th from left. (*Sir David Landale*)

Right: W/O E. P. Lewis in POW camp.

Walker, pilot; P/O R. V. C. Bolster; and Sgts A. S. Carson and A. H. Knape, who all lost their lives.

W/O Lewis was captured, slightly injured, on 28 June and made a POW. He was taken to Stalag Dulag Luft at Oberurfel, near Frankfurt-on Main, where interrogation of captured airmen was carried out. He was then transferred east via Stalag 1X C Dulag A at Bad Sulza, then Luft 3 at Sagan (100 miles south-east of Berlin and infamous for the 'Great Escape' when 50 officers escaped and were recaptured and shot in March 1944). He was then sent to Luft 1 Barth, and finally Stalag Luft V1 at Heydekrug, a POW camp for NCOs near the Lithuanian border in East Prussia, on 25 November 1943. Here he was involved in two escape attempts with a Royal Engineer sergeant. One tunnel reached 40 feet before discovery, and in a second attempt, they escaped and were 200 miles away before capture. In the camps he was known as 'Moley' and 'Finch', as well as 'Ianto' after a character in the book and film *How Green Was My Valley.*

On 3 March 1944, W/O Lewis crawled along a trench into the wash-house which was under repair and strolled out of the camp dressed as a civilian worker. By this time, he was fluent in German and Polish and integrated himself into the Polish countryside, working on lonely farms. At the end of July it appears that he was making for the port of Danzig in East Prussia to gain passage out of the country. Here he followed two Swedish workers through the dock gates. They waved their passes, Lewis waved a piece of paper and walked on. The guard challenged him. He ran and the guard shot him. This account came via the Polish underground. The official record is that the SS shot him on 1 August. It makes little difference. This was a young airman who deserved to succeed.

W/O Ernest Philip Lewis is buried at Malbork Commonwealth War Cemetery, Poland, grave ref: 3.A.4.

Chapter 12

Short Cut to Disaster

Following the fall of France in the summer of 1940, the Luftwaffe soon found bases from which to attack Britain via the Irish Sea where there was less chance of being intercepted than over land. The U-boat fleet could also now operate from ports in western France, straight out through the Bay of Biscay to sink shipping in the northern Atlantic. In the first seven months of 1942, these submarines sank some 589 Allied ships in the area including the Arctic. Our lifeline of supplies, war materials, food and oil was being cut. It was a desperate situation, not to mention the losses of seamen. Help was on the way, though.

U-boats on the surface, when charging their batteries while in transit across the bay, could be detected by a metre wave ASV (Air to Surface Vessel) radar carried by aircraft based in England. In January 1942, Dr Bernard Lovell[1] was given charge of a team to develop a blind bombing system for Bomber Command, H2S, and also a version of this, a centrimetric ASV, for Coastal Command. Coincidentally in 1942, Wing Commander H. de V. Leigh produced a powerful searchlight to be fitted on aircraft – the Leigh Light.

On detecting a surfaced U-boat with the metre wave ASV radar, the Leigh Light was suddenly switched on and depth charges dropped. The shipping losses were soon on the wane, for these aircraft had an alarming effect on the U-boat crews. Every time they popped their heads above the water, or so it seemed, along came a Wellington turning night into day and

---

[1]During 1956/57, the writer worked as a research assistant maintaining radar equipment detecting daylight meteor streams and aurorae under this dedicated scientist, by then Professor Bernard Lovell, director of Jodrell Bank Experimental Station.

determined to sink them. The German navy developed a radio receiver to detect the radar, but soon the centrimentric ASV radar came on stream. This could detect targets as small as a conning tower above the waves. Again, on came the Leigh Light followed swiftly by depth charges. So in the months of April and May 1943, some 56 U-boats were sunk in eight weeks. The end of the submarine was nigh, but the pressure had to be kept up.

In 1943, Liberator GR (General Reconnaissance) V1 four-engined aircraft with long range were fitted with these centrimentric ASV systems and closed the Atlantic gap. On the eastern side of the Atlantic, one of the squadrons operating these aircraft was No. 547 Squadron (motto: *Swift to Strike*) based at St Eval in Cornwall. In the spring of 1944, a new crew joined the squadron skippered by W/O Stan Kearney. Several of them had come together at 111 OTU at Nassau in the Bahamas. Alec Campbell: "The Nassau course was three months, two on twin-engined B-25 Mitchells and a month on Liberators. At the end of the course we were

Above: Stan Kearney and crew at 111 OTU, Nassau. Back L-R: Alec Campbell, Stan Kearney, Sgt A. Beer (not on EV881 flight), Ray Sellors, John Duncan Boyd. Front L-R: Robert Evans, Ted Moody, Billy Soroski. (*George Jared via Pembrokeshire Aviation Group*)

Above: RAF Liberator KG869, 547 Sqn, sister aircraft of EV881.
(*Danny Quinn via Pembrokeshire Aviation Group*)

posted to No. 45 Atlantic Transport Group in Dorval, Montreal. There was more flying in Mitchells, practising radio range flying. We were then ferried back to the Bahamas, where Liberator EV993 had just completed repairs to leaking fuel tanks. After an air test and some sleep we were off to the Azores – then off to Prestwick in Scotland via Lagens. At Harrogate, we waited for a posting which turned out to be St Eval in Cornwall where we went operational around March 1944 with 547 Squadron."

The original crew, W/O Stan Kearney, pilot; F/Sgt Alec Campbell, 2nd pilot; F/Sgt John D. Boyd, RCAF, navigator; F/Sgt Robert Evans, wireless operator/air gunner; F/Sgt Raymond Sellors, flight engineer; W/O Billy W. Soroski, RCAF, wireless operator/air gunner; and W/O Edward Moody, RCAF, wireless operator/air gunner, were now brought up to the complement of ten with the addition of P/O Richard N. Shearly, RCAF as 2nd navigator, Sgt Danny Quinn, air gunner and Sgt Albert H. Humphries, air gunner.

On 18 September 1944, the crew completed a nine-hour anti-submarine patrol, landing at 0315 hours. Even though the crew were stood down, the following afternoon they were alerted to get ready for a flight that evening. They were to rendezvous with a Royal Navy submarine, the next best thing to a U-boat to practise their radar and Leigh Light skills on. Alec Campbell again: "Why we were picked for this exercise I don't know. Perhaps it was because we had been on patrol the previous night and the crew were still together apart from the rear gunner, Danny Quinn, who had gone into Newquay for some dry cleaning. It was a perfunctory briefing to tell us that we were to rendezvous with a Royal Navy submarine in an area to the north of Rathlin Island off the north-east coast of Ireland." The crew, now numbering nine, assembled at their assigned aircraft only to find it unserviceable, so a delay ensued while they transferred to another Liberator – EV881. Instead of flying west and then north to skirt Wales, using the Smalls lighthouse off Pembrokeshire as a fix, the decision was taken to take a short cut across south-west Wales to make up time for their naval appointment.

"We knew we would cross the south-west tip of Wales, but nobody gave any thought to high ground and we were close to the sea. Even so, I was a bit perturbed about hills and switched on the landing lights, but they failed to illuminate any terrain. Immediately after this we crashed. I don't know how, but I was thrown out onto a hillside with EV881 blazing away alongside. I met Ted Moody, the radio operator, who had been seated just

behind me on the starboard side. He said his high padded seat saved him in the crash, then the side of the aircraft opened up and he fell out.

"We tried to obtain entrance to the plane through the rear lower hatch, but there was nobody there. There should have been two gunners standing at the waist gun ports. I guess they were flung forward into the bomb bay. By this time local people were turning up to help.

Left: Memorial to crew of Liberator EV881, Preseli Hills. (*John Evans*)

Above: L-R, the three survivors of Liberator EV881: Alec Campbell, Ted Moody, Dick Shearly with Danny Quinn in the 1987 reunion of 547 Sqn Association.
(*Danny Quinn via Pembrokeshire Aviation Group*)

Someone guided Ted and I down the hill. I thought it was the local vet, but later was told there was no vet living in the area. I woke up in hospital and the next day was flown to a burns unit in an Anson air ambulance."

The Liberator had crashed into Carn Bica on the summit ridge of the Preseli Hills, bursting into flames with the 1,500 gallons of fuel it was carrying. There was only one other survivor – P/O Richard Shearly, the 2nd navigator. The other six of the crew all lost their lives, though F/Sgt Robert Evans lasted up to his admission in hospital.

Dick Shearly: "As we flew north we had no warning of the crash. Johnnie Boyd and I were in the nose. He was navigating and I was to do the first practice runs using the Leigh Light to spot the sub. I passed out like a light and came-to two or three days later in a Welsh hospital. I remained in hospitals and a convalescent home until VE Day." Sgt Danny Quinn had returned from town and was astonished to find his crew missing – flown off without him. He was so disappointed not to have flown with them. In reality he was a lucky airman.

Both Alec Campbell and Ted Moody recovered and rejoined 547 Squadron, which in the meantime had moved to RAF Leuchars in Scotland, to complete their tours of duty. On 19 September 1984, forty years on from that fateful day, a memorial was laid and a service held at the crash site, organised by members of the PAG (Pembrokeshire Aviation Group). Relatives of the crew were among those assembled.

Chapter 13

Saved by the Pony Express

F/Lt Daniel J. Hurley was a wartime pilot with No. 576 Squadron (motto: *Carpe diem – seize the opportunity*) flying Lancaster bombers. This squadron was based at Elsham Wolds from November 1943 to October 1944, when it moved to Fiskerton in Lincolnshire until the end of the war. After his operational tour, F/Lt Hurley was posted to RAF Llandwrog in North Wales, presumably to be a staff pilot to the trainee navigators of No. 9 (Observers) Advanced Flying Unit. Here he met his wife-to-be, Alice, in Caernarfon. Flying came to an end there in June 1945, though many years later it would become Caernarfon Airport. Daniel and Alice moved to Newport where they married in 1946. Remaining a pilot in the RAFVR, Daniel Hurley studied long hours in his spare time to become a commercial pilot. In the early 1950s, he was accepted as a pilot for Cambrian Airways.

The Airspeed Oxford was extensively used to convert pilots to handling twin-engined aircraft. On 12 December 1953, Oxford HM784, attached to No. 3 RAF Reserve Flying School, took off from Filton airfield, Bristol, to fly to Cardiff Airport. The pilot was F/Lt Daniel J. Hurley, RAFVR. When the Oxford did not arrive at its appointed time of 12.30pm, a Coastal Command aircraft carried out a search of the Bristol Channel to no avail.

On that Sunday, Graham McNeil, a 24-year-old colliery worker and his two nephews, David Beynon and Norman Price, were up on Mynydd Carn-y-Cefn, the mountain ridge between the Ebbw Vale and Sirhowy valleys, which reaches over 1,500 feet. They had come to round up horses and take them down to milder quarters in the valley for the winter. The summit was covered in mist so Mr McNeil and the boys split up to search a wider area and arranged to meet later at a prearranged point.

"When I got there the lads had not arrived, so I thought something had

Above: Wreckage of Oxford HM784. The arrow points to the seat where F/Lt Hurley was found. (*South Wales Argos*)

Left: Graham McNeil, rescuer of F/Lt Hurley. (*South Wales Argos*)

Right: F/Lt D. J. Hurley: survivor of Oxford crash. (*Penny Williams*)

gone wrong. There are a lot of crevices on this part of the mountain, and perhaps one of the lads had fallen in one." Visibility was down to around five yards, so he started to whistle hoping to make contact. Then he heard a shout for help. Still whistling, so that the caller could direct him, he moved towards the place where the shouts were originating from.

Suddenly, a heap of aircraft wreckage loomed through the mist. A moment later he found the pilot lying there, his face covered in lacerations. His first words were, "Thank God, you have come." Mr McNeil asked if there was anyone else in the aircraft and was relieved by the reply. An attempt was made to get the pilot on his feet, but he told his rescuer of a pain in his back. He was eased down onto the grass again. F/Lt Hurley then asked if a pipe and a flying boot could be found. The wind was bitter at this altitude. The pipe was found but, as the boot did not appear, Mr McNeil placed a flying glove around the bare foot.

Then out of the mist rode the two nephews. They had heard the aircraft and the crash at 12.15pm and were looking for it. They were sent off to raise the alarm while Graham McNeil found the parachute, deployed it and wrapped it round the pilot to keep his body heat in. When the boys returned, the airman was lifted onto one of the horses which was led down the mountain in the direction of Waunlwyd. Because of his back injuries in particular, this was a most painful journey for the pilot. They arrived at a slag disposal works where the ambulance met them and transported the injured pilot to Ebbw Vale Hospital.

His wife and three young children, twin girls and a boy, visited him the next day. Daughter Penny recalls seeing him covered in plaster from the neck to the pelvis. Graham McNeil visited F/Lt Hurley in hospital a few

days later. He later made a complete recovery but never flew again as a pilot. Citations were sent to the rescuers by G/Capt J. G. L. Read, Officer Commanding No. 63 (Wales & West) Group at RAF Hawarden. The letter to David Beynon includes the words 'It is likely that K/LT Hurley would have died of exposure if he had not been found by you, your uncle and Mr N. Price at the time, and I am very grateful to you for your prompt act of mercy'.

The outcome could have been very different. A day on from the crash there would have been very few people on the mountain until the spring. Although Mr McNeil was able to contribute much of this story, sadly his two gallant nephews both died some years ago.

Chapter 14

Anson v Offa

In May 1995, I answered a knock on the door to find two pleasant-looking men there: Ron Harvey and his son. Ron had a story for me – I did not have to go searching for it. In September 1942, F/Sgt Ron Harvey was a staff pilot at RAF Moreton Valence, south of Gloucester, a satellite of RAF Staverton and base of No. 6 AOS (Air Observers School). On the 13th, he was flying Anson DJ659 along with staff navigator Jack Rodd and three pupil navigators. Low stratus cloud developed from 800 to 1000 feet, obscuring the ground. Then the wireless packed up so they were not able to obtain a position. Harvey decided to descend and look for a place to land. This was done in a small meadow at Smithers Cross Farm, Ruardean, in the Forest of Dean, without injury to crew or damage to the aircraft. A guard was placed until suitable weather should arrive to chance a take-off.

On 21 September, F/Sgt Harvey was detailed to carry out a night cross-country flight, again with F/Sgt Rodd and three other pupil navigators. The final turning point on a leg from Cambridge was to be at Hereford and back to base. Ron Harvey continues, "The weather was filthy, in and out of cloud, pouring with rain. We identified the lights of Wellesbourne and Pershore airfields through a convenient gap in the clouds and Jack gave me a revised ETA at Hereford, five minutes later than the original. Jack managed to contact base again, the wireless having failed half an hour after take-off and we had missed a general recall because of deteriorating weather. The re-established contact made no mention of the recall! We were flying at 2,000 feet, presumed to be over Hereford and, either as we turned onto the final leg or immediately afterwards, we hit something." (The summit ridge of the eastern part of the Black Mountains along which runs Offa's Dyke

Left: Ron Harvey, pilot of Anson N9745, after commission. (*Ron Harvey*)

footpath, part of the 160-mile defensive boundary built for the king of Mercia in the 8th century).

"Solid ground, I knew. We bounced and bounced again, and started skidding, then a sudden spin to the right. Intuitively I knew my starboard engine had found a hole to rest in, and there we stopped. In those few frightening seconds I'd switched off the engines and applied the brakes – the main wheels of the Anson protruded a tyre's depth when the undercarriage was raised... Jack, thinking we had collided with another aircraft, had opened the door, parachute clipped on, ready to get everyone out. However, all was silent. He carefully felt below with his foot and found something reassuringly firm. He climbed out into the blackness, the cloud and the rain, very carefully. It was as well that he did. Immediately aft of the door the fuselage was overhanging (we later saw) a 300 feet sheer drop. Only the weight of the engines had saved us from plunging to our deaths.

"The rest of us followed Jack, and just as warily. We were all intact apart from one of the pupils who had been sitting in the wireless operator's position and had been thrown forward, striking his head on the wireless. He was a little vague and his head wound was bleeding, but kept in check with a handkerchief pad. I was bleeding too, from a gash on my chin, which I'd sustained when my face hit the cockpit roof as we plunged crazily across the mountaintop. We made our plans. I left the three trainees in a safe place near the Anson with strict instructions not to go back in the aircraft or wander off while Jack Rodd and I went for help. The rain was easing off and our eyes had become used to the dark. We could hear the splash of water very close and to the left. Very carefully we crawled towards the sound and found the stream almost immediately. Calling out farewells to the others we started off down the mountain, straining our eyes to see as far as possible and keeping to our steep and watery path. The time was about 11.30pm

"We were soon under the cloud base and were able to look across what appeared to be a valley whilst we rested from our difficult descent. We were not too sure but there appeared to be in the blackness a solitary light level with us in the distance. It must be the light in a window, not blacked out as it should be in wartime. Soaking wet, we carried on following the stream downwards as our spirits soared. In the half-hour it took us to reach the valley floor, we did our best to keep the beacon in view, disappearing now and then behind trees. We arrived at a river about fifteen feet wide. How deep? This is our lucky night: let's chance it! We waded in and reached the far bank, the water having only reached our hips. Emptying our flying boots, we set to find the elusive light, somewhere up the lane alongside the river. On we squelched, feeling more and more optimistic, and then suddenly there was the light within a stone's throw. We threw no stone however, but knocked on the door of this isolated cottage.

"It was ages before the door was slowly opened by a man who'd obviously been having a nap and peered out at us suspiciously. Our story must have been convincing though, for after ten minutes in his tiny living room he volunteered to climb the mountain to rescue the rest of the crew. He claimed, as a shepherd, he knew every inch of the mountains. Indeed, he found them within half an hour and took them back to his cottage.

"In the meantime, Jack and I followed the directions the kindly shepherd had given us to reach the village of Llanthony and a public telephone, just past the *Half Moon* hotel. I telephoned my flight commander at Moreton Valence, who was relieved to hear from me and amazed that we had all survived the crash. We made ourselves known at the *Half Moon* and told our story to the two charming middle-aged ladies who owned it. They directed us to the cottage of the local home guard captain a few minutes' walk back along the lane. He drove us in his little Singer Nine car very competently along the winding lane to the shepherd who had the three pupils sitting cosily in front of a roaring fire. I decided that the injured lad should go to the nearest hospital at Abergavenny for treatment. The captain took us, with Jack and I admiring the way that man handled the car with just his left hand. His right arm had been severed some years before in a farming accident.

"Our injured airman was attended to by the hospital staff who decided to keep him in for a while. We returned to the *Half Moon* hotel. There, after downing a few scotches with our hostesses, Jack and I fell into bed around 4am Mid-morning next day, transport arrived to carry us back to Moreton Valence. There were endless reports to write and questions to answer on the loss of the aircraft. The medical officer recommended that I should take a week's leave. However, my flight commander suggested that I go back to the lone Anson at Smithers Cross Farm and take charge of the airmen guarding the machine. I spent a very pleasant time there, but the wind conditions were never suitable for a take-off. After three or four weeks, the Anson was dismantled and transported back to base on a low loader.

"Years later I heard that Jack Rodd was killed on operations while flying over the English Channel. I went on a tour of operations on Lancasters in 1944, followed by a spell of instructing pilots on Wellingtons and Oxfords until I was demobilised in 1946."

Chapter 15

The Air Training Corps
Museum at Abergavenny

In October 1968, a wartime airman, Des Hemmings, founded 2478 Squadron Air Training Corps at Abergavenny. This followed a wartime squadron based in the town. This earlier one was able to send suitable cadets to a gliding school nearby at Gipsy Lane, Llanfoist, during the war. Des Hemmings had been a wartime airman, giving a false age to become an air gunner a year earlier than the requirement of seventeen and a quarter. He became a flight sergeant rear gunner serving with Nos 217, 214, 76 and 35 Squadrons in turn on Stirlings and Halifaxes before joining 635 Pathfinder Squadron operating Lancasters from Downham Market.

On 26 August 1944, he was on an operational flight to Kiel in Lancaster ND355. The aircraft was hit by flak as they were crossing over the Dutch/German border, which caused the whole of the tail section of the fuselage to break clean away and plunge earthwards with Hemmings in it. As he was unable to rotate the turret to bale out, he made his way to the end of the plummeting tail section and managed to jump clear as he deployed his parachute.

He made a safe landing and for a couple of days evaded the Germans, though he was eventually spotted and taken as a POW to Stalag Luft 1. After the war, Des Hemmings worked for the Irvin parachute company for a while, testing new designs. In 1972, as F/Lt Hemmings, the first commanding officer of 2478 Squadron, he started to collect interesting items of wreckage from the many wartime aircraft that had crashed throughout South Wales. The various items which he and his cadets collected were displayed in a room at the squadron HQ in Trinity Street, Abergavenny. The display of parts of aircraft involved with fatalities may have been controversial, but the majority of visitors had nothing but praise for the museum, highlighting the sacrifices made by the young wartime airmen.

Sadly, Des Hemmings passed away in 1979, but his close friend and colleague Peter Durham took over the museum. He was a civilian instructor for the ATC and threw himself into the job with great enthusiasm. He located and recovered many more items from crash sites further afield. Just as significant, he built up a formidable list of crash information across South Wales from local, RAF and Air Historical Branch sources. This was entered on a card index system and is an invaluable record for other aviation historians and relatives of airmen seeking information including crash sites.

In 1982, Peter Durham collaborated with fellow enthusiast Dewi Jones of Skewen to publish a book privately, entitled *Warplane Wrecks of South Wales & The Marches*. A thousand copies were printed and snapped up. It was an invaluable source for historians and the public alike. With the increasing amount of material coming into the museum, it became necessary to fit new, larger display boards. The curator painted these a light blue, similar to that on the RAF ensign, which brightened up the display considerably after the previous matt black. On 18 October 1990, an open day was held at the museum, which was well attended by the general public who passed many favourable comments. It came as a great shock to everyone when Peter Durham died suddenly on 21 February 1992 after being admitted to Neville Hall Hospital.

W/O Danny Hickey, who had been working closely with Peter Durham, was appointed as the new curator by the then CO, F/Lt Morvan, who also provided a much larger room to house the substantial number of exhibits.

Above: General view of A.T.C. Museum at Abergavenny. (*Len Roberts*)

Danny Hickey personally cleaned hundreds of items and made new boards to mount them on. He also went out further afield as far as Welshpool to search areas in the heart of wild and lonely mountain regions, involving steep climbs and long tiring walks over very rough terrain, to log crash sites and bring back items which would otherwise disappear in time. He was usually accompanied by up to twenty cadets, keen to see parts of an aircraft some of which are not even in museums.

However, another shock came in 2002 when the ATC decided that they did not like the museum and promptly had it closed. The various engines, display boards, exhibits and visual records of aviation history are now hidden away in garages and sheds until the day wives shout "Enough!" Surely an aviation-minded businessman could help out and find a place for the most important displays. The lottery fund also springs to mind. Danny Hickey and his friends would like it to happen after all their effort and hard work. We owe it to those airmen who lost their lives on the mountains.

In the meantime, 2478 Squadron ATC at Abergavenny, aside from their training, continue to provide guards of honour on public occasions and dedication ceremonies held at local churches to remember those aircrew who died. These young men have performed their duties with dignity and are a credit to the town.

Part III

APPENDICES

British Military Aircraft Crashes

Airspeed Oxford

06.01.46. PH242 21(P)AFU. Struck Black Mountains near Offa's Dyke path along the top of Hay Bluff in bad weather. 2 of 3 crew survived. (See *Fallen Eagles*).

06.12.53. HM784 3 RAF RFS. Hit summit of Ebbw Vale Mountain in fog. 1 survivor. (Chapter 13)

Armstrong Whitworth Whitley

13.11.40. T4232 10 Sqn. Hit summit of Rhymney Hill, off course in cloud. 4 survived, 1 killed. (Chapter 11).

04.01.42. K7246 9AGS. Forced landing/engine failure on Gwynian Mtn/Dowlais. Crew all OK.

Avro Anson

17.01.39. L9149 AST Hamble. Struck Bannau Brycheiniog in bad weather. 2 survived, 2 killed.

30.03.40. N9545 Ferry Unit. St Athan to Sealand. Flew low over parent's home. Hit high ground near Machen. 1 killed.

10.07.40. N5019 15 OUT. Lost in bad weather, flew into Y Gamrhiw. 1 survivor, 4 killed.

02.03.40. N9879 6AONS. Lost in bad weather, hit ridge of Black Mountains. 3 survived, 1 killed.

21.09.42. N9745 6AONS. Blown off course, hit ridge of Black Mountains. 5 survived.

15.12.44. EG639 10RS. Flew into Foel Cwm-cerwyn in poor visibility. 2 killed.

Avro Lancaster

05.09.43. W4929 1661 HCU. Struck Rhyd-wen-Fach, north of Fan Foel at night. 8 killed.

10.04.44. JB471 NTU. Broke up after pilot lost control, near Llanwrtyd Wells. 8 killed.

Right: Anson N5019 site on Y Gamrhiw. (*Len Roberts*)

Avro Vulcan

11.02.66. XH536, 12 Sqn. Low flying TFR exercise. Struck Fan Bwlch Chwyth. 5 killed.

Bristol Blenheim

22.09.40. L8610 17 OUT. Flew into Garn Wen in cloud on cross-country flight. 3 killed.

Consolidated Liberator

19.09.44. RAF EV881 547 Sqn. Flew into Carn Bica, Preseli Hills, at night. 3 survivors, 6 killed. (Chapter 12)

De Havilland Hornet

30.09.46. PX273. Struck Mynydd y Glog on cross-country flight St Athan to West Raynham. 1 killed.

De Havilland Vampire

09.10.53. VZ106. 233 OCU. Dived through cloud and hit west side of Fan Hir. 1 killed.

27.10.53. W618 208 AFS. Dived into ground near Rhymney. 1 killed.

12.12.55. VZ871 233 OCU. Collision over Crychan Forest. 1 survivor.

12.12.55. W566 233 OCU

Fairey Battle

26.02.40. K7688 9BGS. Made forced-landing on Preseli Hills. 3 survivors.

Handley Page Halifax

22.08.42. W1238 102 Sqn. Engine failure. Crash-landed near Llanfaredd. 8 survived. (Chapter 9)

23.01.44. DG358 1667 HCU. Engine failure in storm. Crashed at Bryn y Groes. 9 killed.

29.02.44. LW366 420 Sqn. Elevator control rods broke at 20,000 feet. Crashed near *Cross Inn.* 2 crew baled out OK, 5 killed.

22.05.44. LK835 51 Sqn. Engine fire. Crew baled out OK. Crashed in peat bog at Waen Afon. 7 survivors. (Chapter 9)

12.12.44. LL541 1664 HCU. Pilot lost control. Crashed at Nant yr Haidd. 9 killed.

Hawker Hurricane

07.01.40. L2074 11 Grp Pool. After dogfight practice, descended though cloud and hit top of Mynydd William Meyrick.

26.09.41. Z3662 79 Sqn. After dogfight practice, descended through cloud, stalled and crashed into Rhigos Mountain. US pilot. 1 killed.

Lockheed Hudson

07.01.40. N7256 233 Sqn. Test of ASV radar equipment from St Athan. Crashed making forced-landing on Mynydd Maendu.

20.08.41. T9442 233 Sqn. On operational patrol. Navigational error. Hit high ground 3 miles south of Gilfach Goch.

Miles Martinet

31.01.44. MS525 7AGS. Flew into hillside near Port Talbot in bad visibility. 1 killed.

11.08.44. MR614 587 Sqn. Struck 1,000 feet hill in fog near Llanshamlet. 1 killed.

21.12.45. HN888 595 Sqn. Flew into Cwm Bwch in bad visibility. 2 killed.

Miles Master

04.10.42. W8773 5(P)AFU. Flew into high ground near Abergwesyn in formation. 2 killed.

04.10.42. DL570 5(P)AFU. 2 survivors.

North American P-51 Mustang

09.09.45. KH499 112 Sqn. Forced landing on Mynydd y Glog.

Percival Proctor

24.12.43. HM305 4RS. Collision with Proctor HX321. Crashed at Upper Cathedine, Llangorse. Other aircraft landed OK. 2 killed.

12.01.45. NP216 4RS. Flew into Corn Du in cloud. 1 survivor, 1 killed. (Chapter 8)

23.08.45. NP306 4RS. Power loss/engine problem, low flying in Gospel Pass. Forced to land on side of hill. 2 survivors.

Supermarine Spitfire

06.08.41. X4381 53 OTU. Wing came off, dived into hill at Ton Pentre. 1 killed.

12.08.41. R7057 53 OTU. In low cloud, flew into Mynydd Pen y Cae. 1 killed.

03.11.41. X4913 53 OTU. Flew into north face of Pen y Fan. Missing 9 months. 1 killed..

08.03.42. L1014 53 OTU. Seen to dive out of clouds in a spin into side of Skirrid. 1 killed.

23.05.42. X4588 53 OTU. Flew into high ground on Gwaun Nant Ddu in cloud. 1 killed.

08.07.42. R6777 53 OTU. Aircraft exploded in mid-air, crashed Blackhill, Glam. 1 killed.

15.08.42. P8380 53 OTU Lost in rain and cloud. Hit high ground near Cymmer. 1 killed

Vickers Wellington

19.09.39. L4256 75 Sqn. Lost in bad weather over mountains, crew baled out. Aircraft crashed near Pont Nedd Fechan. 5 survivors.

09.12.40. T2520 115 Sqn. Bad weather as squadron returned from raid on U-boat pens at Bordeaux. T2520 struck Cefn yr Ystrad. 6 killed.

08.04.42. R1597 23 OTU. Struck by lightning, crashed near Llangammarch Wells. 7 killed.

06.07.42. R1465 22 OTU. Descended through cloud and struck Waun Rhyd. 5 killed.

25.09.42. BJ697 120TU. Flew into Fan Hir on cross-country night flight. 4 survivors, 1 killed.

29.12.42. R1174 11 OTU. Pilot lost control in cumulonimbus cloud. Crew baled out. Aircraft crashed on Mynydd Tre-newydd. 3 survivors, 2 killed.

20.11.44. MF509 22 OTU. Engine problem plus build-up of ice in shower cloud, aircraft lost height and struck Carreg Goch. 6 killed.

Westland Lysander

21.05.41. V9371 225 Sqn. Searching for lost Tiger Moth in bad weather. Flew into hill near Pembrey. 1 survivor, 1 killed.

31.12.41. R9119 400 Sqn. Engine failure due to icing. Forced-landing on mountainside near Gelligaer, Glamorgan. 1 survivor.

Right: Engine from Martinet HN888, Cwm Bwch. (*Len Roberts*)

Appendix B
Bibliography

Brock, Deric: *Wings Over Carew*; private publication, 1989.

Charlwood, Don: *No Moon Tonight*; Goodall Publications, 1984, 1994.

Charlwood, Don: *Journeys into Night*, Hudson, 1991.

Doylerush, Edward: *No Landing Place*; Midland Counties Publications, 1985.

Doylerush, Edward: *Fallen Eagles*; Midland Counties Publications, 1990.

Doylerush, Edward: *No Landing Place* volume 2;
    Midland Publishing Ltd, 1999.

Durham, Peter & Jones, Dewi: *Warplane Wrecks of South Wales & The Marches*;
    private publication, 1982. OOP.

Evans, John: *Final Flights* volume 1; Paterchurch Publications, 2005.

Jones, Ivor: *Airfields and Landing Grounds of Wales: South*;
    Tempus Publishing Ltd, 2007.

Jones, Steven H.: *Fallen Flyers*; Bryngold Books, 2005.

Lovell, Sir Bernard: *Echoes of War*; Adam Hilger, 1991.

Pearce, Robin T.: *Operation Wasservogel*; private publication,
    (Beaminster, Dorset) 1997.

Roberts, W. J. L.: *Aircraft Crash Sites*; Thirty sites in the Brecon Beacons
    National Park booklet with map from Brecon Beacons National Park Service,
    1996.

Smith, David J.: *Action Stations 3 – Military Airfields of Wales and the
    North-West*; Patrick Stephens, Cambridge, 1981.

Appendix C
Aircrew Memorials

This is a list of memorials to aircrew. Their names are listed in various chapters where the accidents are described.

Avro Anson L9149. GR825214, Fan Brycheiniog. A small stone at the entrance to Callwen Church, Glyntawe, commemorates this crash.

Avro Lancaster W4929. GR828238, Fan Foel on Carmarthen Fans. On 5 September 1993, relatives of those who lost their lives were flown to the crash site in a Sea King helicopter from RAF Brawdy. A service was held and a memorial erected.

Bristol Blenheim L8610. GR285046, Garn Wen near Pontypool. In 2000, the niece of the pilot, along with her husband and willing helpers from Abergavenny, placed a memorial stone at the crash site.

Boeing B-17 Fortress 42-5903, *Ascend Charlie*. GR243253, Pen Gwyllt Meirch. Exactly 50 years from the date of the crash, and at approximately the same time, a memorial service was held at Llanbedr Church. A plaque with the names of the crew was placed on the wall to the left of the entrance door.

Consolidated Liberator (RAF) EV881. GR127318, Carn Bica, Preseli Hills. In 1985, the Pembrokeshire Aviation Group placed a memorial stone at the crash site, visited by relatives of the victims on the 50th and 60th anniversaries of the crash: 1994 and 2004.

Martin B-26 Marauder 41-34765, Carn Llidi, near St David's. A memorial was erected and dedicated in 2005 attended by relatives of the crew.

Vickers Wellington R1465. GR066202 on Waun Rhyd. This crash site is virtually found at the centre of the Brecon Beacons National Park. In 1958, pupils and staff of Tredegar Comprehensive School, clambered up the slopes with sand and cement.

With rocks from the mountain, they constructed a substantial cairn to house a memorial. The crew are not forgotten, for pupils and staff climb the mountain each year to lay poppies in armistice week.

Vickers Wellington MF509, GR817168 on Carreg Goch. There is a memorial stone and plaque with the names of the crew on the site.

The crews of the following aircraft are remembered together: Avro Lancaster JB471, Llanwrtyd Wells. Miles Master W8773, near Abergwesyn. Taylorcraft Auster ES956, Garth. Vickers Wellington, Llangammarch Wells.

The above four aircraft all crashed in what was formerly North Breconshire. On 17 September 1994, a dedication service was held in the church at Llangammarch Wells for the crews, eighteen airmen in all. It was Battle of Britain Day and RAF Valley recognised the service for their own by sending a flypast of four Hawk aircraft.

F/Sgt Trevor Charles Jones (see Chapter 6). A plaque to this airman can be found in St Michael's Church, Myddfai.

Below: Memorial cairn on the site of Wellington R1465. (*Len Roberts*)